*"We earn $4[...]
have [...]"*

*"Our child is 14 . . . and we don't have a
penny put aside for college."*

*"Me, save money? There's barely enough to
make it to the end of the week."*

If any of these statements sound familiar,
you can benefit from the expertise of certified
financial planner Barbara O'Neill. With this
simple, easy-to-follow plan for increasing your
savings and improving your financial situation, you can learn:

- how to find your "financial X"—to assess
  your current situation and figure out
  where you want to go
- how to get the best insurance at the
  lowest cost
- the basics of estate planning
- how to maximize the time value of money
- seven common spending errors
- money do's and don'ts for married couples
  and more

SAVING ON A SHOESTRING

SAVING
—on a—
Shoestring

HOW TO
CUT EXPENSES
REDUCE DEBT
STASH MORE CASH

Barbara O'Neill, CFP

BERKLEY BOOKS, NEW YORK

While a great deal of care has been taken to provide accurate and current information, the ideas, suggestions, general principles and conclusions presented in this text are subject to local, state and federal laws and regulations, court cases and any revisions of same. The reader is thus urged to consult legal counseling regarding any points of law—this publication should not be used as a substitute for competent legal advice.

SAVING ON A SHOESTRING

A Berkley Book/published by arrangement with
Dearborn Financial Publishing, Inc.

PRINTING HISTORY
Dearborn Financial Publishing edition 1995
Berkley edition/December 1996

The Putnam Berkley world wide web site address is
http://www.berkley.com/berkley

ISBN: 0-425-15344-4

BERKLEY®
Berkley Books are published by The Berkley Publishing Group,
200 Madison Avenue, New York, New York 10016.
BERKLEY and the "B" design are trademarks belonging to
Berkley Publishing Corporation.

PRINTED IN THE UNITED STATES OF AMERICA

10 9 8 7 6 5 4 3 2 1

This book is dedicated
to the memory of
my father,
Francis X. O'Neill,
June 25, 1920–February 18, 1993,
who showed me many times that,
with hard work and dreams,
anything is possible.

Acknowledgments

Many authors, especially first-timers, face writer's block as they begin to put their thoughts down on paper. Fortunately for me, this book did not have to begin totally from scratch. Bits and pieces of *Saving on a Shoestring* have been germinating since 1983 as I've studied, researched, taught and written about personal financial planning. My sincere thanks to the following individuals and organizations that have helped me along the way:

- Gene Bronson, my husband, for his love, encouragement and support.
- Mary O'Neill, my mother, for her love and encouragement of every one of my academic endeavors since kindergarten.
- Cook College of Rutgers University (New Brunswick, N.J.), a generous employer that has enabled me to develop and expand my knowledge and professional skills.
- The College for Financial Planning (Denver, Colo.), the National Center for Financial Education (San

Diego, Calif.) and the HIDM department of Virginia Polytechnic Institute and State University (Blacksburg, Va.) for enhancing my knowledge of personal financial planning.

- *The New Jersey Herald* (Newton, N.J.) for providing me the opportunity to hone my writing skills for 16 years and spread the word about the importance of financial planning.

Contents

Preface

This book was written for the millions of people in this country who say they wish they could save some money or increase their current rate of personal savings. Somehow, there just always seems to be more "month" than money. Many of these same people also mistakenly believe that financial planning is something to do *only* when they are wealthy (which they know they'll never be) rather than a process that should be undertaken immediately to accumulate assets for present and future needs and to enhance future security.

Like anything that is done for the first time, the process of financial planning can be intimidating. Just gathering the data required to prepare a cash flow or net worth statement is enough to discourage all but the most financially attuned. Yet, without a financial plan, your money will find its way into hundreds of places besides a bank account.

When your goals are discussed with family members, written down and clearly described, you'll start finding ways to reach them and make a greater effort to save money for those things that are important to you. A case in point is my husband, who, when given a choice, prefers spending to saving any day. For the past few years, we've taken a winter vacation in the Caribbean. Saving $30 each per week in a Christmas club provides the $3,000 we need for the trip and we really don't miss the money.

In 1991, the median income for U.S. families was just under $36,000. Households within $10,000 of this amount (up or down)—the middle-est of the middle class—are the target audience for *Saving on a Shoestring*. Most people in this income bracket don't have large lump sums of money to save or invest. They do have two other very important resources; their *earning ability* and—for all but the aged—*time* for their savings to earn interest on interest through compounding. With proper planning and a bit of discipline, people of average means can achieve financial independence and retire in comfort.

Does this sound too good to be true? It's sometimes hard to believe that there's such a thing as financial independence when there are three days until payday and you're broke. You can stretch your money, however, if you know what you want to do with it and where it presently goes. Getting in the habit of spending by choice (to be explained in detail later) and managing credit wisely are other prerequisites for financial success.

One of the most common financial errors people make is procrastination, also known as the "I meant to's." Have you meant to prepare a will, for example, or purchase disability insurance or transfer existing savings dollars from a passbook bank account to a higher yielding bond or mutual fund? The best financial plan in the world is worthless without corresponding action to implement it. Still, many people do not take the steps necessary to turn their dreams into reality. In 1973, the personal savings rate in this country was at an all-time high of 9 percent. During the second quarter of 1993, it was only 4.5 percent. A widely quoted study released in 1993 found that the average baby boomer saves only a third of the amount needed to fund a comfortable retirement.

Saving on a Shoestring was written to inspire action. It is a tool that can change your financial life—if you want it to. Chapter 2 will help you clarify your goals and develop a plan of action to achieve them. In Chapter 5, for example, you'll find a list of 25 ways to save money. In Chapter 6, you'll learn how to spend by choice and live well on less. Chapter 7 will help you develop a spending plan that works because it reflects your personal values, goals, income and expenses.

Notice that I used (and will continue to use) the phrase *spending plan* instead of the word *budget*. This was intentional. Like the word *diet*, *budget* is often perceived negatively. It has come to be associated with deprivation or denial in the minds of many people. Financial self-discipline, however, does not necessarily mean self-denial. Instead, it is the putting off of small, often insignificant pleasures now to experience greater, more important ones in the future.

To continue the analogy with between weight control and spending, financial planning is a combination of both willpower and action. One of the most important aspects of any financial blueprint is a spending/savings plan for day-to-day and future expenditures. Financial planners refer to a regularly scheduled savings habit as "paying yourself first." Savings is treated with the respect given to major bills, like a car loan or mortgage payment, and part of each paycheck is set aside immediately—while you still have the money.

Are you paying yourself first? Even if you have only spare change, start saving something now—today. Don't wait until your car loan is repaid or your children leave home or you get that promotion at work! The sooner you start saving, the sooner your money will grow. Time management experts often talk about "swiss-cheesing" a task, or poking it full of holes (small, manageable steps). Start to think of your financial goals as a piece of swiss cheese. For example, if you need $2,000 in a year and get paid biweekly, saving $75 each pay period will achieve this goal.

Above all, begin to nurture a positive attitude about your finances. Reject thoughts of failure and turn obstacles into challenges. Try to envision yourself enjoying the achievement of all your financial goals. Think about it. Perception is reality. When you think positively and take positive action, you'll achieve the best for yourself and your family.

1

Why We Should Save Money and Why We Don't

"We earn $40,000 a year and have only a $500 savings account."

"This year we earned $5,000 more than last year and had to borrow to pay our income tax."

"Our child is 14 and we don't have a penny put aside for college."

"Me save money? There's barely enough till the end of the week."

Do any of these statements sound familiar? These words (and many others) are often uttered by persons with little or no savings. Did you ever do your income taxes and wish that you had more to show for the gross income you earned? When asked what they would have done differently with their money during the 1980s, 51 percent of almost 3,000 respondents to a 1992 *Money* magazine survey said they would have borrowed less, two-thirds said they would have saved more and 54 percent said they would have invested more.

The rate of household savings has been below historical averages for about a decade and is currently well below its peak in the early 1970s. Between 1980 and 1991, Americans saved 6.4 percent of disposable personal income, compared with 15.7 percent for Japan. In 1992, the personal savings rate was 4.8 percent, about three to four times less than both Germany's and Japan's. Although accounting methods and demographic characteristics account for some of the savings gap, the difference is still striking.

Small wonder that Americans say they are worried about their financial future. Many households have little to fall back on. According to one recent estimate, 70 percent of Americans live paycheck to paycheck, courting disaster if their incomes are interrupted or reduced. The recommended emergency fund of three to six months' expenses is a pipedream for many families.

For savings to become a reality, it must be treated as a regular expense and given top priority. This is called paying yourself first and Chapter 5 will show you how. If your child were sick, your car needed repairs or you wanted to send flowers to a relative's funeral, you'd find the money somehow, wouldn't you? Perhaps you'd cut back on your food bill that week or readjust other monthly expenses or postpone a purchase. Saving money for future goals is just as important. As the saying goes, "Where there's a will, there's a way."

10 Good Reasons To Save Money

① **To Generate Income**—Regular savings can build a sizable nest egg, which, in turn, can be tapped to provide income to meet normal living expenses. A pool of savings is especially important for retirees who need to use personal funds to supplement Social Security or employer-provided retirement benefits. A monthly investment of $50 will have grown to almost $30,000 after 20 years, assuming an average return of 8 percent compounded monthly. Savings of $100, $250 and $500 monthly, at the same interest rate, will be worth $59,295, $148,240 and $296,475, respectively, after 20 years.

② **To Meet High-Cost Future Goals**—Among the most expensive goals that individuals and families face are the purchase of a home, a college education and a comfortable retirement. The funds needed for each are substantial and must be planned (and saved) for early. To purchase an average home, for example, buyers often need to cough up a down payment of 10 to 20 percent of the purchase price plus another 3 to 6 percent of the amount borrowed for the closing costs. To buy a $120,000 home with a $100,000 mortgage may require savings of up to $25,000 to close the deal. Naturally, the more savings (or equity in a prior home) that a homebuyer has, the smaller the mortgage that he or she will require.

Saving for college requires almost as much money, if not more. According to the College Board, an organization that tracks educational expenses, college costs have increased faster than the inflation rate for more than a decade. The average 1993–94 school year costs for public and private colleges were $8,562 and $17,846, respectively, with tabs of more than $25,000 for a handful of private and prestigious schools. Parents who haven't kept track of college costs since their own student days often experience "sticker shock" when their children reach adolescence.

The sooner you start saving for your child's education, the less you'll need to save per year. For example, a four-year college that costs $9,000 a year now will cost about $80,000 when today's five-year-old is ready to attend. The annual savings required to accumulate $80,000 when a child is 5, 10, and 15 years old is $3,720, $7,520 and $24,615, respectively, assuming an 8 percent rate of return.

③ **To Retire Comfortably**—A comfortable retirement will require even more money than college or a home but, fortunately, the window of opportunity to save is much wider. The savings period can be as long as 40 years if someone starts setting aside funds at age 25 and chooses to retire at age 65. Assuming no current retirement savings plan is in place, let's look at a married couple, both 35 years old, planning a $50,000-a-year retirement (in today's dollars) at age 65 for an assumed joint life expectancy of 20 years. Let's also assume that they'll each receive $9,000 annually from Social Security and another $10,000 each in employer retirement benefits (these figures are also in today's dollars).

In the above scenario, there exists a $12,000-a-year shortfall. Therefore, in order to retire comfortably, the couple will need to set aside just under $4,000 a year from now until retirement, assuming an average after-tax return of two percentage points above inflation. If they wait to start retirement savings until age 45, 55 or 60, the required annual savings jumps to $7,850, $17,650 and $37,280, respectively, which, of course, is more than most middle-income households can manage (particularly if they're simultaneously paying for one or more col-

lege educations). Persons who are not entitled to receive
employer benefits naturally must save more than their
peers who will collect a pension.

④ **To Cope with Emergencies**—Sooner or later,
most people face at least one emergency, including—but
not limited to—the following:

- A broken furnace (usually on the coldest day of winter)
- Septic system malfunction
- A sick family member
- A broken car or appliance
- Disability due to accident or illness
- The death of a friend or relative who lives far away
- Unemployment (due to downsizing, layoffs, etc.)
- A substantial amount of money due the IRS
- Damage to home (from flood, fire, vandalism, etc.)

Savings provides a cushion against life's emergencies.
For this reason, most financial planners recommend setting aside at least three months' expenses in a liquid savings instrument such as a passbook savings account,
money market fund, NOW or SuperNOW checking
account or short-term certificate of deposit (CD).
Liquidity is the ability to readily convert an asset to cash
without loss of principal.

Families with only one wage earner may wish to consider increasing their emergency fund to as much as six
months' expenses because they have no second paycheck
to fall back on. Persons planning to leave a salaried position to start their own business should have 6 to 12
months, expenses in reserve.

⑤ **To Purchase Big-Ticket Items**—While many people manage to pay for small purchases with current income, this is difficult to do when the product or service in question costs several hundred (or several thousand) dollars. Examples include a major appliance, a vacation, a new car, a daughter's wedding reception and home improvements such as a deck or a fireplace. By swiss-cheesing a goal (poking it full of holes by breaking it down into smaller, manageable steps) and saving an amount that fits your income, big-ticket items need not always be purchased with loans or a credit card. For example, if you'd like to make a $7,500 home improvement in three years, saving about $200 a month will provide the needed funds.

⑥ **To Build a Cushion for Planned Changes in Family or Career**—For any number of reasons, individuals or families can find themselves living on less income than they once did. Sometimes a pay cut is planned and sometimes it is unexpected. Examples of planned reductions in income include quitting a job to go to school or to start a business, changing careers and scaling back to live on one paycheck so that a spouse can leave his or her job to raise young children full-time.

The more advance preparation an individual or a household has for its plans, the easier its transition will be. A person or a household can start saving immediately to have on hand a healthy percentage of the amount of after-tax income that it would have earned. A young middle-manager netting $25,000 annually, for example, might sock away $4,000 to $5,000 a year for a few years if he or she has plans to take a leave of absence from work to enter a full-time MBA degree program.

⑦ **To Establish Security and Peace of Mind—** Having a financial cushion is good for the psyche. It's much easier to sleep at night when you know that you're not a paycheck (or a heartbeat) away from insolvency and that your money won't run out before the month does. People with an emergency fund are in a better position to handle life's financial crises. A successful savings program also contributes to a euphoric sense of being in control, which can reduce stress levels. Instead of your money managing you, you manage your money!

⑧ **To Outpace Inflation—**It is a sad but true fact of life that inflation reduces the purchasing power of a dollar. At an average annual inflation rate of 4 percent, prices will double approximately every 18 years. If the inflation rate were to increase to 6 or 8 percent, prices would double in only 12 or 9 years, respectively.

Saving money at an interest rate greater than or equal to the rate of inflation, therefore, increases (or, at the very least, maintains) purchasing power. You can use a simple formula to find the rate of return (RR) that is needed to break even after taxes and inflation. Simply divide the expected annual inflation rate by 100 minus your marginal tax bracket. For example, let's assume a 5 percent average annual inflation rate and a 15 percent and a 28 percent tax bracket saver:

15% $RR = 5 \div (1-.15) = 5 \div .85 = 5.9\%$
28% $RR = 5 \div (1-.28) = 5 \div .72 = 6.9\%$

These savers would have to receive almost 6 and 7 percent, respectively, on their money in order to maintain purchasing power. If they earned more, they'd be keeping ahead of inflation. A realistic average return for most people to aim for on their total portfolio is 1 to 3 percent above the breakeven rate.

⑨ **To Generate Investment Capital for Long-Term Growth**—It is often not possible to earn 1 to 3 percent above the breakeven rate on conservative bank savings products. Moreover, the potential for growth is nil and the income earned is fully taxable. Persons looking for long-term growth, a higher rate of return and tax advantages generally set their sights on investments such as stocks, bonds, mutual funds, annuities and real estate. But where do these people get the money for their initial (and subsequent) investments? Unless they've received a windfall of some sort, the money probably comes from savings.

If you can save $2,000 a year ($38.46 per weekly paycheck) in a money market fund paying 4 percent and leave both the principal and the interest intact, you'll have about $10,800 in five years. Keep at least three months' expenses in savings products that can be quickly turned into cash, and the rest of the money can be diversified among a variety of higher yielding investments.

⑩ **To Aid the Country**—In addition to high bankruptcy rates and family debt problems, Americans' low annual savings rate has alarmed politicians and economists for a rather global reason: savings provides the capital needed for economic growth and expansion. The money that individuals and businesses place in financial institutions is invested in factories, business expansion, building projects and research that can lead to new technological break-throughs.

During the 1980s, foreign investors began filling in the gaps when domestic savings were insufficient to finance all of the public and private investment needs of the country. Today, many foreigners own substantial amounts of real estate, stock and treasury securities, which exacerbates the skittishness of the international money market.

5 Bad Excuses for Not Saving

① **The Cost of Living Is Too High**—While it's true that few major household expenses decrease from year to year, high living costs are simply not a reason to throw up your hands in despair and decide that saving money is not worth the effort. Lack of money is often more of an *excuse* than a real reason not to save. More often than not, people don't save money because they lack motivation or discipline or both.

Many financial planners advise saving 10 percent of your gross income. It's easy to compute and is certainly an admirable goal. Many families, particularly those with young children or four-digit monthly mortgage payments, are simply unable to save this much. So be it! It's far better to save 2, 3 or 5 percent of your income than to save nothing at all. As family expenses decrease (or income increases) in the future, the amount of money allotted to savings can be upped by a percentage point or two a year.

② **There's Nothing Left To Save**—This phrase illustrates, once again, the lack of priority that many people attach to savings. If you think you lack the discipline to make a savings deposit each pay period, get someone to do it for you! You can arrange for direct deposit of your paycheck into a bank account or deductions from your salary into a credit union or an employer savings plan.

③ **The Government Made Me Do It**—It is true that government tax policies have tended to reward consumption and discourage savings. Up until 1986, interest charges incurred for any purpose were fully deductible as an itemized tax write-off. Today, as in the past, mortgage interest is deductible on first and second homes, thereby encouraging investment in real estate, often in lieu of other types of savings and investments. Moreover, money placed in savings continues to be taxed in *at least two* places—first, when it is earned as income and, second, on the interest or dividends it generates (and, if you have enough, it might also be taxed a *third* time as part of your estate).

Not surprisingly, blaming the government is a convenient excuse for not saving, although it really doesn't hold much water. Today, numerous tax-free and tax-deferred investment products and devices, such as trusts, allow taxpayers to keep more of what they earn. In addition, the 1986 tax reform law phased out the government's "subsidy" of consumer debt. In short, saving is "in." The nation's savings rate could reach as high as 10 percent by the late 1990s as baby boomers repay their household-formation debts and enter their peak earning years.

④ **I'd Rather Spend My Money Now**—One reason that we, as a nation, save so little is that we spend a lot. Unless you can increase your income, you'll need to spend less to save more. But how? If you like to spend money, make this habit work *for* you rather than *against* you. Use it as part of your planning and motivation. Set a savings goal and build in your own reward system. Challenge yourself to exceed the goal and treat yourself to a spree with all or part of the excess when you're successful. For instance, if you plan to save $2,000 a year and actually save $2,500, go ahead and spend the extra $500. You've earned it! Next year, set your goal at $2,500 and reward yourself if you save $3,000.

⑤ **I'm Not Sure Where To Put My Money**—Many people avoid decisions about where to put their savings by never leaving themselves any money to save. This is a mistake. Saving money need not take a lot of time or effort. You can keep things simple by starting out with a basic bank savings account. After you've accumulated about $500, switch to a money market fund or CDs if you can earn a higher rate of return. You might also consider an interest-bearing checking account or U.S. savings bonds, both of which can be purchased at a local bank. When your nest egg has increased to several thousand dollars, you'll probably want to contact a brokerage firm or no-load mutual fund to diversify your assets.

Pay Yourself First

Ask any financial planner how people can increase their personal savings rate and you're likely to hear this

phrase: Pay yourself first. This means immediately setting aside (or having someone else set aside for you)
something from each paycheck as soon as you receive it
rather than waiting to see what, if anything, is left at the
end of the month. In short, it is the exact opposite of how
most people handle their money.

To successfully pay yourself first, you need an incentive. Let's look at your current spending habits. What bills
do you unquestionably pay first and on time? If you're
like most people, you probably treat your rent or mortgage payment or your car loan payment with the utmost
respect. Why? The consequences of *not* paying these bills
mean the loss of your home or car! What are the consequences of not paying yourself first? A loss of all the savings advantages listed earlier in this chapter (emergency
fund, peace of mind, inflation hedge, etc.). The consequences of not saving are the loss of the *security* and the
opportunity that a nest egg provides.

Getting started is the hardest part of paying yourself
first. Staying motivated runs a close second. The most
logical place to start is with your goals and cash flow.
Paying yourself first works best when clearly defined
financial objectives mesh realistically with a household's
discretionary income after taxes and major expenses.

The 10 Percent Solution

How would you like to have a nest egg of more than
$40,000 in ten years with almost no work or deprivation
on your part? This is not a phony investment scheme but
rather the amount a median-income family can accumu-

late by diverting 10 percent of its yearly earnings to an investment paying 6 percent. Saving 10 percent of your income can mean the difference between achieving your financial goals and never getting started.

The median household income in the United States was $35,939 in 1991. Ten percent of that is $3,594. If that amount were deposited each year in an investment yielding an average of 6 percent, in ten years the investor would have $47,300.

A lot of people would say that there's no way they could save $3,594 a year (about $70 a week). Maybe yes, and maybe no. The trick is to go over a list of household expenses and circle with a red pen specific items that can be reduced by 10 percent. Take the grocery bill, for instance. An average family of four spends about $136 a week on food. Ten percent of that is a mere $13.60, or an annual savings of $707.

The next time you go food shopping, take a good look at what's in the cart before checking out. Are there expensive snack foods and convenience foods that you could do without or make yourself? Are you buying anything that might end up in the garbage because nobody really likes it? Apply the same tactic to other household expenses. Cut back on utility costs, for example, by following two important energy conservation rules: lights out when nobody needs them and thermostat down at night and when nobody is home. Chapters 5 and 6 will provide additional money-saving ideas.

In summary, few things in life come guaranteed—not a job, a home, a marriage, a college education or the future. Most everything that is important requires effort to achieve and maintain. Even if they're not guaranteed, your financial goals and dreams are worth striving for. In fact, you're not likely to achieve your objectives unless you do strive for them. Saving and investing your money carefully and consistently is the best way to help turn your dreams into reality.

2

First Things First—Defining Your Values and Goals

Did you ever wish that money grew on trees? Then, when the mortgage was due, you could pick off $600. On your way to the supermarket, you could pick another $100. When the electric bill came, money would be there. Unfortunately, money doesn't grow on trees. Most of us have to work for it and plan for future financial needs. It's easy to get caught up in day-to-day living and never look ahead. But you can't achieve financial independence unless you think about and plan for the future.

What exactly is financial independence? The singer Johnny Paycheck alluded to it in his famous song "Take This Job and Shove It." Quite simply, financial independence is a stage in a person's life when he or she is comfortable and totally self-sufficient and needs no job, relative or government for support. Unfortunately, a study several years ago found that 95 percent of Americans who retired at age 65 were not financially independent. Advance planning is a must to maintain a standard of living for decades amidst inflation, tax law revisions and unforeseen changes in both personal circumstances and the economy.

Despite the obstacles, some Americans manage to become financially independent each year without the state lottery, casinos, a big inheritance or a successful business or invention. How? The answer, quite simply, is planning. Some maximize participation in employee savings and retirement programs. Others invest in stock or real estate. Still others save and invest slowly and steadily until their portfolios reach six-figure, and even seven-figure, numbers.

It has been said, "If you don't know where you are going, any road will get you there." This saying applies to your finances. If you don't have a plan for achieving specific goals, the long-term results may be disappointing. It is unreasonable to expect savings accumulation or financial growth without goals and a plan for obtaining them.

What Do You Value Most?

Before you can turn your dreams into reality, you need to think about the things that are truly important to you. These ideals and principles by which we live are known as values. Listed in Figure 2.1 are 25 values that are frequently mentioned. Choose the values that are *most* important to you and place an *A* beside them. Place a *B* by those that are *somewhat* important. Place a *C* beside those that *are not* important.

Now compare the list with your lifestyle and your checkbook. How many *A* items are reflected in your daily activities? Are you spending money on the things that are really important? Do you and your spouse agree on most of your spending values or does your spouse want to buy expensive name-brand products, for example, when you would prefer more inexpensive versions and a family night out with the money saved? It's hard enough for one person to decide which items are most important. It's even harder when two or more people who share money must decide where it should go.

Remember that all decisions, financial or otherwise,

Figure 2.1 What Do You Value Most?

Below is a list of 25 values arranged alphabetically. Study the list carefully. Prioritize the values with the letters *A* (most important) to *C* (least important). Take your time and think about your decisions. The results should show how you feel about the values that guide your life.

❏ comfortable life

❏ community service/volunteer activities

❏ culture (movies, theater, etc.)

❏ earning a lot of money

❏ education/knowledge

❏ excitement/stimulation

❏ family activities

❏ family vacation

❏ friends

❏ happiness/contentment

❏ health

Figure 2.1   What Do You Value Most? (Continued)

❏   image/personal appearance

❏   independence/autonomy

❏   job success

❏   large investment portfolio

❏   new home or condo

❏   prestige/social recognition

❏   recreation

❏   reducing or eliminating debt

❏   religion

❏   security

❏   sense of accomplishment

❏   shopping/spending money

❏   starting/maintaining own business

❏   top-of-the-line products and services

are based on values. Values determine what is desirable or has worth and are influenced by family members, the mass media, life experiences, peers and the culture of the society in which we grow up. Values can make people feel either comfortable or uncomfortable. If you live with people having a different value system, you may feel uncomfortable when standing up for what you really believe in. It's difficult to relax when you're constantly defending your values.

That's why it's important for people who share a

household to communicate openly about spending priorities. If a couple or family agrees on a decision, there is some degree of commitment and a better chance of achieving financial goals.

What Are Your Goals?

Now that you've analyzed your values, let's talk about your goals. Goals are the concrete evidence of your values. They indicate to the world what your value system is. Financial goals are the specific things that you want to do with your money.

It's not enough, however, to just *think* about your financial goals. It is important to write them down so you can see what you say you want. If you don't describe your goals fully, you're less likely to take action to achieve them because they'll remain vague notions in the back of your mind.

Each financial goal that you write down should be realistic and attainable. Goals should also be easy to measure, with a deadline and a dollar cost. This will help you evaluate your progress and plan more effectively. For example, if you need a new car costing $8,000 in three years, saving about $50 a week will provide the needed cash. Be specific. "I plan to save $50 a week for three years" is more detailed than "I plan to save money." Below are a few more examples of goals that have both an estimated cost and a deadline:

- Establish an $8,000 emergency fund within two years
- Provide three children with four years of a public col-

lege education at today's cost of $10,000, beginning in the years 1998, 2001 and 2003

- Have a retirement income of $40,000 a year in today's dollars in the year 2018
- Have $20,000 in the bank by your 40th birthday
- Take a course next semester to improve your job skills and qualify for a promotion
- Buy a car for $15,000 in three years
- Make a will by the end of the month
- Increase your net worth by at least 5 percent a year
- Pay off the $3,000 balance on your charge cards by the end of the year
- Have $10,000 set aside to start a business in five years

Financial planners often refer to three goal time frames: *short term* (less than three years away), *intermediate term* (three to ten years away) and *long term* (more than ten years away). This helps you determine how much time you've got to save. It does *not* mean, however, that long-term goals are less important than short-term ones or that you should postpone saving for them. As noted in Chapter 1, long-term goals like retirement and college education are expensive.

Because of the time value of money (interest compounding on interest over time), a little money saved now for long-term goals can actually exceed a lot of money saved later. To illustrate this point, let's compare two sets of parents of college freshmen. Kara's parents started saving $1,000 a year for her education right after she was born. Jason's parents waited until he was ten and then started saving $3,000 a year for eight years. When Kara and Jason turned 18, their college funds, assuming an average annual return of 8 percent, were worth $37,450 and $31,910, respectively, even though Jason's parents actually saved more money. Time and money are truly a magical combination!

In Figure 2.2, you'll find spaces to list both the cost and the time frame of your financial goals, along with a statement of the actions needed to achieve them. A common goal, buying a car, is given as an example.

Figure 2.2 Evaluate Your Financial Goals

Use your worksheet below to list your financial goals. Categorize your goals according to the time frames suggested earlier (short, intermediate and long term). Determine a date and an approximate cost for each goal and the action steps that you can take to achieve it.

Goal	Time Frame	Date and Cost	Action
Example: Buy a new car	Intermediate -term goal (three to ten years)	$15,000, to be pur- chased in five years	Save $3,000 a year, or $115 per biweekly paycheck
_____	_____	_____	_____
_____	_____	_____	_____
_____	_____	_____	_____
_____	_____	_____	_____
_____	_____	_____	_____
_____	_____	_____	_____
_____	_____	_____	_____
_____	_____	_____	_____

Before you can begin to develop a financial plan, you must establish goals. Goals give a sense of direction and help target the amount of money you need to save. Goal setting forces you to put your dreams down on paper. Once your goals are listed, you'll start developing strategies to reach them. The goal-setting process is exciting because it works. Goals can motivate and inspire you. As soon as they are written down, they become real. If you have more goals than money to fund them, don't worry. You are not alone. Simply list your goals by priority (not in chronological order) and fund the most important ones first.

Many people have a plan in place to cope with circumstances that arise after their death. It's usually in the form of life insurance or a will. Yet so few have a plan for what they'll do while they're alive. What do you want out of life for you and your family? You must know where you are now and where you want to go before you can develop a plan to get there.

The Rule of 72

At this point, you're probably asking yourself what a car, house, college education or cruise, for example, will cost in the future when you're ready to buy these products and services. You're wise to wonder because, unfortunately, the price tag of your financial goals will increase while you're saving the money to achieve them. You can't use today's prices in Figure 2.2 because the future cost of your goals will be higher than today's cost. Inflation is a sad but true fact of life.

To quickly calculate how fast prices will rise, use the rule of 72. This rule can be applied any time you have a fixed sum of money or a current price and want to know how many years it will take to double at a given (or an assumed) interest rate. To calculate, simply divide 72 by the interest or inflation rate. For example, if you assume a 6 percent average annual inflation rate, costs will double in 12 years (72 divided by 6). Today's $15,000 car will cost about $30,000 in 12 years, about $22,500 in 6 years or about $18,750 in 3 years. The rule of 72 gives a ballpark estimate of the amount of money you'll need to save for future financial goals.

You can also use the rule of 72 to estimate the future growth of your savings. If you have a $10,000 certificate of deposit (CD) earning 6 percent, for example, it will double to $20,000 in 12 years (72 divided by 6). If you know only your deadline, divide that number into 72 to find the interest rate needed to achieve your goal on time. For example, if you want to double your money in ten years, you'll need to earn 7.2 percent (72 divided by 10). If you want to double your money in five years, you'll need to earn 14.4 percent (72 divided by 5). The higher the interest rate, the faster your money will double.

Funding your long-term financial goals early in adulthood will mean a significantly greater accumulation of money. The rule of 72 proves this handily. A single $2,000 investment at age 25 will be worth

- $4,000 at age 34
- $8,000 at age 43
- $16,000 at age 52
- $32,000 at age 61
- $64,000 at age 70

Assuming an 8 percent average annual return, the lump
sum doubles every nine years (72 divided by 8). If you
wait until age 34 to save the first $2,000, you lose the last
compounding period, which is the biggest increase.

What Is Financial Planning?

Financial planning and your next vacation have a lot in
common. Let's say you want to travel to Europe. To save
time, you visit a travel agent to make the necessary
arrangements. The first thing your travel agent will want
to know is your destination. Questions about the time
allotted for your vacation and the type of accommoda-
tions (first class, coach, etc.) are also routine.

Another important piece of data is your point of depar-
ture. Which airport will you leave from? The itinerary
can't be completed unless the travel agent knows both
where you are starting out and where you are going.

A financial plan, like your trip, also needs some dollar
figures. That's why you listed your goals and investigat-
ed the current and future cost of funding them. When
you're finished with both your vacation plans and your
financial plans, you should know where you are presently, where you want to be, how long it will take to get
there and how much it will cost.

Financial planning, very simply, is the process of
defining your financial goals and developing and implementing a plan of action to achieve them. A good financial plan is actually a collection of *six* individual plans: a
cash flow/spending plan to manage day-to-day and
future expenses; a **risk management plan** to protect

against large and unexpected losses; an **investment plan** to acquire assets for future goals; a **tax management plan** to reduce federal and state income tax liability to its lowest legal limit; a **retirement plan** to accumulate and maintain assets that provide retirement income; and an **estate plan** to transfer assets to heirs orderly.

The cash flow plan forms the basis for all other financial plans. It's the tool households use to pay day-to-day expenses and set aside money for future financial goals. It's also the place to "reality test" your goals and analyze your assumptions. If you find that you have little money left to save after paying your bills, revise your goals or adjust your income or expenses.

During the late 1970s and 1980s, interest in financial planning increased dramatically. What peaked Americans' interest in planning for the future? Below are five major factors:

① **Inflation**—In the late 1970s and early 1980s, inflation escalated rapidly. Incomes often did not keep pace with price increases.

② **Interest Rates**—Inflation caused interest rates to rise. While savings accounts continued to pay low rates, banks loaned money at 12 to 18 percent. CDs and money market mutual funds paid substantially more than savings accounts and became the first "planning" many people did.

③ **Increased Taxes**—As inflation pushed people into higher tax brackets, income taxes took more money off the top. People began to look for ways to defer taxes or shelter income.

④ **Increased Incomes**—More women began to enter the labor force and their salaries made an impact on family income. As incomes grew, households had more disposable income to manage.

⑤ **Information**—Magazines such as *Money* began publication. Newspapers and television began to offer more information on financial planning topics.

More and more, people are starting to see that ignoring their finances is costly. This cost is not only economic, such as higher taxes or a large exposure to risk, but also includes the emotional stress brought on by reduced financial security.

Are You Financially Fit?

Financial fitness involves many of the same principles as health and wellness. Like a diet and exercise program, a financial plan must match your goals and lifestyle. You must discipline yourself, stick to your plan and measure your progress on a regular basis.

Like an annual physical, a financial plan should be reviewed at least once a year or sooner if conditions warrant. Changes in tax laws and economic conditions and personal events such as marriage, death, divorce or the birth of a child all require periodic revisions of your financial plan.

If you haven't undertaken a financial physical in a while, give yourself a quick examination now. Figure 2.3 lists 20 questions to help you get back in shape. If you answer yes to *all* of the questions, you're financially fit, at least for now. Maintaining fitness will require periodic reviews and revisions of your financial plans. You must monitor them frequently to make sure they still achieve your objectives. If you answer no to several or more of the questions in Figure 2.3, don't despair! You are not alone. These questions, which indicate a lack of activity, provide a good starting point for changes in your financial regimen. As a follow-up, Figure 2.4 lists 35 common financial errors to avoid.

Figure 2.3 Give Yourself a Financial Check-Up

1. Have you made a list of specific financial goals and determined when you want to achieve them?
   _____

2. Have you started a savings or an investment program to fund long-term goals such as retirement or a child's college education? _____

3. Do you have at least three months' expenses in a readily accessible account?_____

4. Is the after-tax yield on your savings and investments greater than the current inflation rate?_____

5. Do you earn interest on your checking account? _____

6. Are your savings and investments diversified? _____

7. Do you consider your knowledge of financial planning topics current? _____

8. Does your spouse know as much about family finances and recordkeeping as you do (and vice versa)? _____

9. Do you know how much you spend and save per month? _____

Figure 2.3 Give Yourself a Financial Check-Up (Continued)

10. Is your monthly income greater than your monthly expenses? _____

11. Do you save money from each paycheck? _____

12. Do you know your net worth? _____

13. Are you paying off high-interest loans and credit cards as quickly as possible? _____

14. Do you have a disability insurance policy that will pay at least 60 percent of your annual salary until retirement? _____

15. Are your life, health and property adequately insured (benefits large enough to cover a catastrophic loss)? _____

16. Do you know your marginal federal income tax bracket? _____

17. Have you estimated your income taxes for the upcoming year? _____

18. Do you have at least one tax-deferred savings or investment product (e.g. individual retirement account—IRA)? _____

19. Do you know what your retirement benefits (Social Security, pension, etc.) will be and how much additional money you'll need to retire comfortably? _____

20. Do you have a recently reviewed will? _____

Figure 2.4 Common Financial Errors

1. No goals or plan

2. Planning too late for long-term goals

3. Failure to carry out financial plans

4. Incorrect or unrealistic estimates of living expenses or the cost of financial goals

5. Not knowing how money is spent

6. Inadequate emergency fund

7. Poor financial recordkeeping

8. Failure to monitor the performance of savings or investments

9. Not realizing that all savings and investments have some amount of risk

10. Placing savings in low-yield products that don't keep pace with taxes and inflation

11. Inadequate diversification of assets

12. Making investments that don't match knowledge or risk tolerance level

13. Failure to save money for retirement in tax-free or tax-deferred products

14. Not participating in employer-provided savings plans where contributions are matched by employer

15. Becoming sentimental about an investment or acting emotionally without considering all the facts

16. No use of leverage in investing

17. Relying too much on financial professionals

Figure 2.4 Common Financial Errors (Continued)

18. Not getting financial advice when needed

19. Squandering a windfall

20. Underinsuring a home or its contents

21. Inappropriate or inadequate insurance

22. Failure to shop for the best interest rates on loans, mortgages, credit cards and savings products

23. Not establishing an individual credit identity

24. Carrying a revolving credit card balance for disposable items such as meals eaten out or vacations

25. Large amount of debt for your income

26. Failure to legally take advantage of income tax laws

27. Insufficient use of tax-favored investments

28. Incorrect income tax withholding

29. No will

30. Incorrect titling of property owned with others

31. Lack of communication about money matters with family members

32. Assuming that someone (e.g., a family member or the government) will take care of you

33. Ignorance of the time value of money

34. Failure to update knowledge of financial planning topics

35. Procrastination

Oops—Your Attitudes Are Showing

Did you know that the words *financial planning* are perceived negatively by some people? In fact, people often develop opinions or harbor preconceived notions about things that can interfere with or limit the positive actions that they could potentially take in the future. While some of these attitudes may be based on past experiences or poor service by persons in the financial services industry, many are based on erroneous assumptions.

One of the most common erroneous assumptions that people have about financial planning is that you have to be rich to plan. In reality, just the opposite is true. While financial planning is often thought of as something you do *after* you have accumulated a lot of money, it *should* be looked upon as something you do *to* accumulate money. Everyone needs some sort of financial plan, whether a person develops it on his or her own or hires someone to prepare it.

Other people avoid financial planning because they're not sure how to locate financial advisers to help them. The way to overcome this problem is to shop around. Interview financial professionals until you find someone you think is competent, honest and experienced and someone with whom you feel comfortable. Many financial advisers give a free initial consultation. If they don't, you can usually interview them somewhat over the telephone.

Inertia is another common attitude problem. It's easy to put off or ignore the need for financial planning when no crisis requires immediate action. Most of us would rather live our lives on a day-to-day basis than cope with a distant and unknown future. Furthermore, financial plans are not always fun. While they may include a new car or a Caribbean vacation from time to time, they must also provide for death, disability and emergencies.

A final attitude that inhibits financial planning is a reluctance to put savings in products that pay more than a minimal return, even if it means losing purchasing power, over time, due to inflation. Some people don't want to make a mistake and are paralyzed by fear. They refuse to educate themselves about personal finance, preferring to continually plead ignorance. By taking no action, these people avoid the stress of decision making.

Remember, everyone has both positive and negative attitudes. They're part of life. Depending on what the attitudes are, they can help or hinder your financial progress. When negative attitudes are replaced with positive action, your financial goals will be closer to reality.

Gathering Financial Records

- You're about to sell your car and can't find the owner-ship certificate.
- You're summoned for a tax audit and can't find all the receipts for your deductions.
- You're appointed executor of a deceased relative's estate and can't find his or her will and life insurance policies.
- You've sold a house and need to determine your capital gain for income tax purposes.

If any of these situations sounds familiar, you've probably learned firsthand the importance of organized financial records. Good recordkeeping is an essential component of the financial planning process. No matter how modest your home, you need a special place to keep your papers. It can be as elaborate as a room or home office or as simple as a corner of the kitchen or a desk drawer. Regardless of the filing system used, review your records periodically and discard items no longer needed.

Two home files, in addition to a safe-deposit box at a bank, are recommended: an active file and a long-term storage file. In addition to holding documents such as insurance policies, the active file should contain unpaid bills, recent paid-bill receipts, recent canceled checks and income tax working papers. After one to two years, those items that are no longer needed should be moved into long-term storage. Below are lists of must-save documents and where they should be stored.

- **In a Safe-Deposit Box**—Birth and baptismal certificates, citizenship papers, marriage certificates, adoption papers, divorce/separation decrees, copies of your will (the original should be filed with your attorney or executor), death certificates, deeds, titles to automobiles, household inventory, photos or videotape of your home and its contents, military discharge papers, bond and stock certificates, important contracts, government-recorded papers (e.g., copyrights and patents).
- **In Active File**—Tax receipts for current year, unpaid bills, paid-bill receipts, recent bank statements and canceled checks, income tax working papers, employment records, health benefit information, credit card

information, insurance policies, copies of your will, family health records (e.g., immunizations), appliance manuals and warranties (for as long as you own the appliances), receipts for items under warranty, inventory of and key to safe-deposit box, loan statements and payment books, passports, net worth statement, list of important family financial data.

- **In Long-Term Storage File**—All needed active-file papers more than two years old; receipts for the purchase, improvement and sale of your home(s); IRA records, especially if the contribution is nondeductible; stock and mutual fund dividend and capital gain reinvestment statements; back-tax records for at least three years (some experts advise holding them for six to eight years).

In Figure 2.5, you'll find a form on which to list important financial data about you and your household. Fill it out and share a copy with your spouse or a trusted friend. It is important that at least one other person understand your recordkeeping system in case of an emergency.

Many people spend more time planning their next vacation than they do their financial lives. Do you, too, spend hours making calls, collecting brochures and reading maps? Do you spend as much time planning your finances? Remember that the most important destination we all share is our future. While any number of roads will get us there, a planned itinerary will make the trip smoother and the future more secure.

Figure 2.5 Important Family Financial Data

Complete the questions that apply to your family situation.

I. Family Information:

1. Your age _____   Spouse's age _____
   Number of family members_____
   Ages and identification of dependents (e.g.,
   son, age 12; mother, age 83) _____

2. Marital status:
   ___single   ___married   ___divorced
   ___engaged   ___separated   ___widowed

3. Employment status:
   How many adult wage earners are there in your
   family? _____
   Their employment status is* _____ part time
   _____ full time   _____ self-employment
   _____ more than one job per family member
   *If there is more than one wage earner, please indi-
   cate the employment status of *each*.

4. Income:
   Total family *earned* income* (e.g., salaries)
   $_____
   Total family *unearned* income* (e.g., dividends and
   interest) $_____
   Social Security income, if any $_____
   *Use your gross income on last year's tax form as a
   guide.

5. Goals: List *in priority order* short-term goals and
   expected expenditures (next three years).

   _____

   _____

   _____

Figure 2.5   Important Family Financial Data (Continued)

List *in priority order* intermediate-term goals and expected expenditures (three to ten years in the future).

_____

_____

_____

_____

List *in priority order* long-term goals and expected expenditures (more than ten years in the future).

_____

_____

_____

_____

6. Investment priorities:
   Why do you want to invest? Divide these reasons into 100 points:

   _____ % hedge against inflation
   +_____ % tax reduction
   +_____ % current income
   +_____ % future growth
   +_____ % safety of principal
   = 100%

7. Time Availability:
   How much time do you have to devote to money management?
   _____ I have ample time to manage my financial affairs.
   _____ I have time only for important decisions.
   _____ I have little time to devote to my finances.

Figure 2.5 Important Family Financial Data (Continued)

8. Risk Tolerance Level:
   How would you describe yourself as an investor?
   _____ very conservative
   _____ willing to assume some risk to achieve
   financial gain
   _____ very aggressive

9. What are your major concerns when considering
   your financial future? (Indicate your order of importance by number.)
   _____ building wealth
   _____ increasing current income
   _____ providing security for my family
   _____ reducing my tax liability
   _____ providing for retirement
   _____ planning for future needs (e.g., education,
   leisure activities)
   _____ hedging against inflation
   _____ providing liquidity for sudden cash needs
   _____ finding an easier way to manage my
   finances

II. Property Ownership Information:

Do you:
   a)_____rent $_____amount of monthly payment*
   b) own your home $_____amount of monthly
                                 payment*
   *Please indicate whether payment includes utilities,
   insurance or taxes.
   $_____original mortgage note $_____note balance
   $_____current market value of home (approximately)

   Do you own additional investment property?
   If so, explain _____
   Net profit or loss per month_____

Figure 2.5   Important Family Financial Data (Continued)

Do you have an outstanding auto loan?_____If yes,
indicate monthly payment(s) $_____ Number of pay-
ments left_____ What is the total of all your average
monthly expenses? $_____Is there money set aside for
savings? _____
If yes, how much? $_____

III. Tax Information:

Do you itemize deductions on your tax return? _____
Did you have a refund or tax bill due of more than
$500 last year? _____
Using your most recent federal income tax return, list
the following amounts:

Gross income	$_____
Adjusted gross income	$_____
Taxable income	$_____
Total tax due	$_____

IV. Insurance Information:

1. Life insurance: (term, whole life, universal life, etc.)

Person Insured	Policy Owner	Face Amount	Type of Policy

2. Disability Insurance:
Do you carry disability insurance?____ If yes,
indicate person(s)
insured_____;
monthly coverage_____; payer of premium_____;
elimination period of months____; and length
of period of coverage ____

Figure 2.5 Important Family Financial Data (Continued)

3. Health Insurance: (Blue Cross/Blue Shield, major
   medical, dental, etc.)

Person(s) Insured	Type of Policy	Payer of Premium	Limit of Coverage

4. Auto Insurance:

Property Insured	Property Coverage	Payer of Premium	Special Provisions

5. Homeowners Insurance:

Property Insured	Property Coverage	Payer of Premium	Special Provisions

6. Liability Insurance:
   Do you carry excess liability (umbrella)
   insurance? ____
   If yes, indicate amount of coverage
   $_____

7. Comments or concerns about your insurance
   coverage. _____
   _____
   _____
   _____

Figure 2.5 Important Family Financial Data (Continued)

V. Retirement Information:

1. Are you retired? _____Yes _____No

2. If yes, indicate your sources of retirement income.

    _____
    _____
    _____
    _____

3. If no, in what year would you like to retire? _____

4. Describe below the sources of retirement income you expect to receive (e.g., Social Security, government pension, IRA, Keogh plan, 401(k) plan, 403(b) annuity)

Person Covered	Type of Savings	Annual Contribution	Payer of Contribution

5. Do you have an IRA? _____ Does your spouse have an IRA? _____

6. What are your retirement lifestyle expectations?

    _____
    _____
    _____

VI. Estate Planning Information:

1. Do all adults in the family have a will? _____Yes _____ No

Figure 2.5 Important Family Financial Data (Continued)

2. If no, explain_____
   _____
   _____
   _____

3. When was the last time you reviewed the will(s)?
   _____

4. If you have children, have you established a
   Uniform Gifts to Minors Act account (UGMA) for
   them?_____ Yes _____No

5. Do you have any trusts established? _____ Yes
   _____ No
   If yes, indicate type and beneficiary (e.g., marital
   trust, spouse).

   _____
   _____
   _____

VII. Miscellaneous Information:

Indicate below any information you feel would help
explain your financial situation (e.g., health problems; child custody settlements; unemployment;
special insurance policy riders, floaters or endorse-
ments; employee savings plans; business interests;
anticipated promotions or inheritances).

_____
_____
_____
_____
_____

3

Determining Your Financial X

If you've ever gotten lost along a busy highway, you've probably gone to a rest stop for directions. Many rest stops have large wall maps to guide disoriented travelers. The maps show an entire state or region, with a large X indicating the location of the rest stop. By checking the map, travelers can see where they are currently and which roads constitute the best route to their destination,

When planning your finances, a net worth statement is your financial X. It tells you your current location, financially, and provides a starting point for the journey to future financial goals. Without a net worth statement, it is difficult to know where you are now and how to best proceed in the future.

Do you know how much money is in your wallet right now? According to several polls, a surprising number of people can give the right answer—to within a dollar. When asked whether they know their net worth, however, most people are clueless. Reasons for never calculating net worth include lack of time, inclination and know-how. Net worth is simply how much you are worth in dollars and cents and it is often likened to a snapshot of your financial activities.

Continuing the snapshot analogy, a good example of how net worth can change is the late billionaire Sam Walton of Bentonville, Arkansas, founder of the chain of Wal-Mart stores. Walton lost more than $135 million (on paper) in 1987 as a result of the stock market crash and his net worth declined significantly (even for a billionaire). His company's stock rebounded in 1988, however, and Walton retained his ranking that year as the wealthiest person in America.

Calculating your net worth by means of a net worth statement (also known as a financial statement or a balance sheet) is a relatively simple process and shouldn't take more than an hour or two. With financial records organized and at hand, first list all your assets at their actual or estimated fair market value. Next, make a similar list of all your liabilities (money owed to others). Net worth is then calculated by subtracting the sum of your liabilities from the sum of your assets.

Once you've calculated your net worth, resolve to perform this financial check-up at least once a year, around the same time each year, to closely monitor your progress. Aim to increase your net worth at least 5 percent annually. Net worth statements are especially valuable when used comparatively. The winter months are, perhaps, the best time to calculate net worth because fewer outdoor chores and activities occupy your time and because tax records are current and readily available.

In addition to establishing a starting point for financial plans, a net worth statement serves as a

- record of your financial progress (or lack thereof) if calculations are done regularly;
- record of property ownership and value of insurance planning and claim purposes;
- list of assets and liabilities needed for drawing up a will or settling an estate;
- prepared financial statement, needed when you apply for a mortgage, loan or credit card;
- measure of a household's emergency savings, debt load and home equity;
- measure of investment diversification, growth and liquidity;
- planning and decision-making tool for financial advisers who assist you; and
- record of retirement savings (e.g., vested pension benefits and IRA contributions) to date.

Remember, net worth can be increased in a variety of ways, not just by saving money. Pension plans funded by an employer provide an increase in net worth as money invested in a plan multiplies. As evidence of the substantial accumulations possible, the monetary value of a pension plan is considered part of a person's gross estate for tax purposes and is subject to division in a divorce proceeding. If you own a home, that, too, is probably increasing in value. Home-ownership is a commonplace way for individuals and families to increase their net worth, which is why some people consider their mortgage a forced savings plan.

Another way to increase net worth, albeit indirectly, is through personal skills and educational experiences, such as a computer course or a college degree program.

People who develop their human capital increase their potential to earn more income. New skills can lead to new job opportunities, which can eventually increase net worth. Of course, the real money you put into a savings account or investments is also an important determinant of net worth. Ten tips for improving your net worth are listed at the end of this chapter.

Your Assets

To begin your net worth statement, list the value of your assets on the left-hand side of a sheet of paper. Figures should be as precise as possible and as of the same approximate date. Separate your list into three types of assets: cash and cash equivalents, invested assets and use assets (personal property).

The **cash and cash equivalents** category includes liquid assets such as

- brokerage cash management accounts;
- cash on hand;
- CDs a year or less in maturity;
- money market deposit accounts;
- money market mutual funds;
- passbook or statement savings accounts; and
- regular, NOW and SuperNOW checking accounts.

These are the types of products in which your emergency fund of at least three months' expenses should be placed. All provide periodic statements and should be easy to value. Also, be sure to include money that you have lent to others if you expect the loan to be repaid soon.

Invested assets are set aside for longer time periods and include

- cash value life insurance;
- CDs with over a year before maturity;
- collectibles;
- corporate bonds;
- 401(k)s and other salary-reduction retirement plans;
- Ginnie Maes and other federal agency investments;
- gold, silver, gems and other precious metals;
- investment real estate;
- IRAs;
- Keogh plans (for the self-employed);
- land;
- limited partnerships (real estate, natural gas, etc.);
- municipal bonds;
- mutual funds;
- ownership interests in a business;
- pending gifts or inheritances;
- profit-sharing plans;
- real estate investment trusts (REITs);
- stock;
- stock bonus plans or ESOP (employee stock owner-ship plan) accounts;
- tax-sheltered annuities;
- unit trusts;
- U.S. savings bonds;
- U.S. treasury securities (bills, notes, bonds); and
- vested pension benefits.

To calculate the value of securities, use the most recent quotes in the financial press or call your broker for an exact figure. Pensions and other employer-provided retirement plans generally send periodic statements to participants and life insurance cash value is listed in a policy or included with premium notices. Specialized investments, like antiques, land or coin collections, generally require professional valuation by a trained appraiser.

The third category, **use assets,** includes

- art and antiques;
- boats;
- cars;
- collections (stamps, coins, baseball cards, etc.);
- home furnishings (appliances, furniture, etc.);
- personal property (clothing, jewelry, etc.);
- small business equipment; and
- vacation property.

Be sure to calculate the value of use assets at *today's* market value and not at their original or replacement price. Values must be conservative, not sentimental. Clothing, cars and furniture generally start to depreciate from the moment you buy them. Clothing should be valued in a net worth statement at no more than 10 to 20 percent of its original purchase price. The value of cars can be determined from local classified ads or guides to used-car prices published by the National Automobile Dealers Association. To value your home, consult For Sale ads in the newspaper or check with a local real estate agent. Many offer free market analyses whether you're planning to sell your home or not. Be sure to subtract from your estimate any taxes or real estate commissions that might be owed upon a sale.

Your Liabilities

A net worth statement is incomplete without a similar list of liabilities. On the right-hand side of your sheet of paper, write down everything that you owe. Include in this section

- car loans;
- college education loans;
- credit card balances;
- debts owed to others;
- home equity loans;
- home mortgages;
- installment loans (furniture, appliances, etc.);
- loans against an insurance policy;
- margin loans on an investment;
- personal loans;
- pledges to charity;
- second mortgages;
- small business debts; and
- taxes and bills due within a week.

The balance owed on all debts and any interest accrued as of the date of the net worth statement constitute your liabilities.

When you've totaled your liabilities, subtract the sum from the sum of your assets. The result is your net worth, or the amount you would have if you turned everything

you own into cash. If you own more than you owe, you
have a positive net worth. If the reverse is true (as is often
the case with college students whose loans are greater
than the value of their possessions), you have a negative
net worth. Once you have a final figure, it's fairly easy to
update it each year and use your net worth statement to
analyze your financial situation.

One interesting net worth analysis is to compare your
car's current value to the balance on the loan used to purchase it. With rapid depreciation on most cars and longer
term car loans becoming the norm, many car owners find
themselves, at least temporarily, upside down, or experiencing negative equity. This means that their car is worth
less than their loan balance. If the car had to be sold, they'd
have to come up with the difference to pay off the loan.

Different types of ratios derived from a net worth
statement also provide helpful insights. By dividing
cash and cash equivalents by liabilities (excluding a
mortgage), a household's ability to handle its obligations can be ascertained. For example, if Joan and Jim
Smith have $30,000 in liquid assets and $5,000 in nonmortgage debt, their liquid-asset-to-debt ratio is
$30,000 divided $5,000 or 6. This means they have six
times as much money as necessary to satisfy their creditors. Sue and Sam Brown, on the other hand, have
$5,000 in liquid assets and $10,000 in debt. Their liquid-asset-to-debt ratio is $5,000 divided $10,000, or .5,
meaning they have only half as much money on
hand as they have borrowed. Any ratio exceeding 1 is
considered good and any ratio exceeding 3 is excellent.
In this example, the Smiths are obviously in the preferred situation.

In Figure 3.1, you will find a sample net worth statement and, in Figure 3.2, a blank form to complete your own financial statement. See Figure 3.3 for some additional factors to consider as you analyze your own net worth.

Figure 3.1 The X. Ample Family

Net Worth as of July 1, 1994				
Assets:			**Liabilities:**	
Cash and Cash			Visa card (8)	$ 200 jt
Equivalents			Car loan	3,055 jt
Cash	$ 100	jt	Mortgage	64,700 jt
NOW checking			Home Equity	7,800 jt
account	1,550	jt	loan (9)	$75,755
Money market				
fund (1)	3,000	jt		
CD #1 (2)	3,240	h		
CD #2 (3)	5,350	w		
	$13,240			
Invested Assets				
Growth mutual				
fund	$ 4,380	jt		
Stock (4)	2,240	h		
Life ins.				
cash value	1,200	w		
Life ins.				
cash value	2,650	h		
Vested pension				
value	10,210	w		
IRA #1 (5)	12,640	h		
IRA #2 (6)	13,580	w		
401(k) plan				
value (7)	12,500	h		
	$59,400			

Figure 3.1 The X. Ample Family (Continued)

Assets: (Continued)			Liabilities: (Continued)	
Use Assets				
House	$125,000	jt		
Cars	11,000	jt		
Household furnishings	10,000	jt		
Personal property	8,000	jt		
	$154,000			
Total Assets:	$226,640		**Total Liabilities:**	$ 75,755
			Net Worth:	$150,885

Footnotes

jt = joint: h = husband; w = wife
(1) Check-writing privilege; interest rate fluctuates
(2) Matures 12/18/96; pays 5.61 percent
(3) Matures 4/16/97; pays 4.52 percent
(4) Purchased through husband's employee stock bonus plan
(5) Invested in CDs yielding 4.3 percent to 6.5 percent
(6) Invested in a self-directed brokerage account
(7) Balance from payroll deductions since 1990
(8) Paid in full each billing cycle
(9) Interest rate charged is two points above prime rate

Figure 3.2 Personal Net Worth Worksheet

Net Worth as of _____ **(date)**
Indicate the type of asset, its current value and its owner.
Example: bank CDs—$1,000 (h); XYZ stock—$500 (w);
house—$80,000 (jt).

Assets: **Liabilities:**

Cash and Cash   (e.g., mortgage, car loan,
   Equivalents   credit cards, family loans)

_____   _____
_____   _____
_____   _____
_____   _____
_____   _____
_____   _____
                                             _____

Invested Assets

_____
_____
_____
_____
_____

Use Assets

_____
_____
_____
_____

Total Assets: $_____   **Total Liabilities:** $_____

Footnotes   **Net Worth:** $_____

Figure 3.3 Analyzing Your Net Worth

---

1. Have your assets and liabilities increased or decreased during the past year?
2. Are you asset rich due to inflation but low in liquidity?
3. Which assets and liabilities do you own individually and which do you own jointly with a spouse or another person?
4. How does the value of your investments compare with previous years?
5. How does the equity in your home compare with previous years?
6. How much money have you accumulated for future financial goals?
7. How much diversification do you have?
8. Have you established an adequate emergency fund?
9. How much cash value, if any, is accumulated in insurance policies?
10. Have you taken on longer term debts, such as a mortgage or home equity loan?
11. Are you using long-term debt (e.g., a home equity loan) to finance depreciable assets (e.g., a car)?
12. Is your net worth keeping pace with inflation? That is, does it increase at an annual rate greater than or equal to the inflation rate?

Financial planners often use footnotes and ownership labels to further explain items in a net worth statement. You should, too. For instance, you might list a CD as one of your assets and use a footnote to specify its interest rate and date of maturity. Other uses of footnotes include due dates on loans and any other information not disclosed in a net worth statement that pertains to stated assets and liabilities.

National Averages—How Do You Compare?

Have you ever wondered what families similar to yours in size, composition and income level spend on such things as food, housing and vacations? Of course you have! It's perfectly normal to want to compare how your own household expenses stack up against others. A better way to compare households, however, is to analyze net worth statements. After all, the Jones family up the block who owns the Jaguar and takes seven vacations a year might just have taken out a substantial home equity loan and reached the limit on all of their credit cards. They may not be wealthy at all! The Smiths, on the other hand, increase their net worth gradually through savings and the judicious use of credit. They don't mortgage depreciating assets and they don't charge vacations and restaurant meals. Who is in the better financial position? Don't look at their lifestyles; look at their net worth statements. A net worth statement is the best indicator of a household's financial status.

So how does your net worth compare with others' net worth? According to the Bureau of the Census, the median household net worth in the United States in 1991 was $36,623. That is, half of all households had a greater net worth and half fell below this figure. Household net worth decreased from $41,472 in 1988, mainly as a result of declines in home equity, checking accounts, rental property and assets held in businesses.

Government figures also indicate that home equity accounts for the largest share of net worth. The second most important asset type is interest-earning assets such as bank checking and savings accounts. Not surprisingly, home mortgages compose the largest household debt.

What do all these statistics mean? Very simply, an increase in the value of assets or a decrease in the amount of debt improves your net worth. Over time, the results can be dramatic. What *really* counts are not the flashy car, the designer clothes and the luxury products and services that just about anyone with a credit card can buy today but rather the things that most people can't see: an emergency fund, tax-deferred retirement savings plans, home equity and a nest egg available for future financial goals.

What Is Wealth?

If you ask people what their ultimate financial goal is, many would say, "I want to be wealthy." Comparisons to someone like Donald Trump or a recent state lottery winner are not unusual. Most people, however, have no idea what wealth *really* is or how to achieve it. It remains a vague, albeit pleasant, fantasy.

Many people believe that wealth can be achieved only through a large income. This is not necessarily true. Many people who make $80,000 to $100,000 or more each year live paycheck to paycheck just like others who earn a fraction of their income. In fact, many of these "wealthy" people show up at Consumer Credit Counseling agencies seeking relief from their creditors and a plan for future spending.

On the other hand, people of average means can, and do, retire in comfort. They plan ahead and build wealth through some of the invisible assets, like a company savings plan, mentioned earlier. Between 1985 and 1991, the number of millionaire households in the United States increased more than 60 percent, from 1.3 million to 2.1 million.

A high income provides an opportunity to accumulate wealth but does not automatically make anyone wealthy. If you earn $80,000 a year and spend $85,000, you will eventually go bankrupt. If, however, you earn $35,000 and save $3,500 a year for 35 years in a product earning 8 percent, you'll accumulate more than $600,000. Now *that's* wealth!

Another common myth about wealth is that it must be shown off with status symbols such as a 5,000-square-foot home or a three-week cruise. As noted previously, "things" don't necessarily prove that anyone is wealthy and, in fact, can work against the accumulation of assets. If the bulk of your income is committed to a high four-digit monthly mortgage payment or the repayment of previously accumulated debt, there will be little money left to save.

This is not to say that wealthy people don't have fun. Most do. Their fun, however, comes as a result of their accumulating assets and becomes one of their financial goals. Spending money on "things" is fine as long as other important financial goals are not sacrificed in the process. Very often, the difference between barely surviving and emerging affluence is planning and a positive attitude.

10 Tips To Improve Your Net Worth

When you calculated your net worth, were you shocked by the numbers? Many people are pleasantly surprised to see that their net worth is higher than they thought. You may also be wondering why, if you're worth so much, it's so difficult to get ahead. Below are ten tips to keep your net worth growing in the future.

① **Act On Your Goals**—The clearer the goal, the more likely you are to attain it. Looking ahead can force you to make plans and take action that will improve your net worth.

② **Earn Money on Your Money**—Unless your savings is earning enough to compensate for both inflation and taxes, you are losing money.

③ **Take Advantage of Tax Laws**—Good records should be kept throughout the year to ensure maximum use of tax deductions and credits. Maximum advantage should also be taken of tax-deferred retirement savings programs.

④ **Insure Wisely**—Spend the bulk of your insurance dollars to insure against large losses such as the loss of a wage earner's income, disability, liability and the total destruction of your home.

⑤ **Diversify Your Assets**—Reduce investment risk by placing small amounts of money in several places rather than in any one type of investment. Even a selection of more than one mutual fund is advisable. Never put all of your eggs in one basket!

⑥ **Shop for Financial Services**—Watch for advertisements by financial institutions. Compare the services offered and the fees charged. Avoid institutions that charge a multitude of high fees, such as per-check charges and fees for the use of automatic teller machines.

⑦ **Prioritize Your Spending**—Make a list of items you really need and concentrate your spending on needs rather than wants. Only you can tell the difference. Don't buy anything on sale, no matter how inexpensive, if you don't need it, can do without it and never intended to buy it before seeing it on sale.

⑧ **Read the Fine Print**—Never make an investment without completely reading the prospectus and getting all of your questions answered. If an investment makes you uncomfortable or you don't understand it, it's not right for you.

⑨ **Take Advantage of Time**—Many people wait too long to start funding long-term goals. Unless you begin saving early, you lose the tremendous advantage of interest compounding on interest over time.

⑩ **Educate Yourself About Money**—Keep up to date on changing tax laws and new investment products through financial publications, seminars and the media. Consult financial professionals, when needed, for specific advice and to implement your financial plans.

In summary, hardly a business or an institution in this country does not prepare an annual financial statement. It is important for investors, management and government regulators to regularly review their financial progress. While households usually don't run their affairs like a business, they, too, need periodic reviews. Remember, though, that a net worth statement alone is no guarantee of future success. It simply tells you where you are today and how you've spent your money thus far.

4

Now You See It, Now You Don't—How To Track Your Cash Flow

Cash flow is a term used by financial planners to describe the delicate balance between income and expenses. End a month earning more money than you've spent and you've got positive cash flow. End up in the hole and you've got the reverse. Households with a consistent pattern of negative cash flow are either depleting their savings or using borrowed funds and credit cards. More about that in Chapter 9.

Many people today are experiencing financial difficulties instead of enjoying a sense of financial security. Their problems range from the relatively small (e.g., a $100 car repair) to the seemingly insurmountable (e.g., prolonged disability). Financial problems are often the result of failure to manage money effectively, regardless of income.

Some people today earn a six-figure income and barely make it. If they were unemployed or disabled for more than a few weeks, they'd be in serious financial difficulty. If you consistently spend more than you earn, you will eventually lose everything. This is why a spending plan is so important. It may not be fun but it sure beats the alternative! *Spending plan* is an action-oriented synonym for the word *budget*. When most people hear the word *budget*, they immediately think of the three Ds—denial, deprivation and don't—or the three Cs—cutback, cutout and can't. Their good intentions are shot down before they begin. Like the word *diet, budget* triggers feelings of negativity and resistance. It almost feels like we're being punished by someone. *Spending plan*, on the other hand, emphasizes personal control. A spending plan, very simply, is a plan for saving and spending household income. When people feel like they are in control, their plans are more likely to succeed.

Getting a handle on your cash flow is an important part of developing a spending plan because it is difficult to know what adjustments to make if you don't know where your money goes. A cash flow statement shows how much money a household earned and spent during a given time period. While keeping detailed records for a month or two to see where your money goes is tedious, the potential benefits of financial security and goal attainment make it well worth the effort. Gathering data is an essential component of the financial planning process. Unfortunately, it can also discourage people from starting to plan their financial future. To make the process less of a chore, consolidate the necessary records ahead of time and coordinate calculations with a related task, such as filling out college financial aid or income tax forms.

Actually, you can't afford *not* to keep track of your finances. Why? Because it costs too much in terms of both time and money. The hours spent trying to document tax-deductible expenses a year or two after they are incurred are lost forever, not to mention the higher tax bill that will most likely result. Ignoring the cost of items purchased with credit will result in high interest charges and a bad credit rating if bills are chronically paid late. These are just a few of the problems that can result when people fail to pay attention to where their hard-earned money goes.

Like a balance sheet, a cash flow statement shouldn't take more than a few hours to prepare. The better your financial records and the shorter the time period being tracked, the easier it will be. If you've never before completed a cash flow statement, start by keeping track of all your income and expenses for one *typical* month. Avoid the holiday season, when expenses and income are likely to be skewed. Then try tracking one or two more months or, if you're up to it, an entire year. The more tracking you do, the more complete a picture you'll have of your finances.

The first figure you'll need to list is your cash balance at the beginning of the time period being tracked. Next, list all sources of income, whether they are taxable or not. Child support or a cash birthday gift, for example, need not be reported for income tax purposes but should be listed on a cash flow statement. Finally, make a similar list of all expenses, including savings (remember the pay yourself first concept). Cash flow is then determined by comparing the sum of income to the sum of expenses.

Once you've prepared your first cash flow statement,

subsequent ones shouldn't take as long because you'll already know your expense categories and the amount spent on major items like a mortgage. Remember, however, that a cash flow statement alone will not change your financial life. It is not a spending plan. A cash flow statement simply increases awareness of current income and expenses and how the two numbers compare.

Your Income

To begin a cash flow statement, divide a sheet of paper into two sections—one for income and one for expenses. Next, list the starting balance and the source and amount of all income in the appropriate section. For simplicity (and to avoid math errors), round off all figures to the nearest dollar. Be sure not to overlook windfalls and irregular sources of income, such as quarterly interest or dividends. Sources of income that should be listed on a cash flow statement include

- alimony;
- annuity payments;
- bonuses;
- business, farm or free-lance income;
- capital gains on investments (e.g., a mutual fund);
- cash gifts (e.g., birthday, Christmas);
- cash prizes and awards;
- child support;
- commissions;

- dividends (from investments and insurance);
- expense account reimbursements;
- gambling proceeds (e.g., bingo);
- garage sale or flea market proceeds;
- honorariums;
- inheritances;
- insurance claim settlements;
- interest on savings;
- lump-sum distributions (e.g., pension) used for income;
- proceeds from the sale of property;
- public assistance;
- refunds and rebates;
- rental property income;
- retirement savings withdrawals and distributions;
- royalties;
- salary or wages;
- scholarships;
- Social Security;
- tax refunds;
- tips; and
- unemployment and disability benefits.

Be sure to calculate your income accurately and completely. To arrive at the exact figure that you received, you may need to refer back to copies of tax returns, paycheck stubs, bank and brokerage account statements and your checkbook. Better still, set up a daily log or diary. This will help you track your income and develop an awareness of exactly how much money is at your disposal.

Your Expenses

After you've totaled your income, list your expenses. Tracking expenses is more complex than tracking income because you have more categories to consider and fewer written records to refer to. Many household expenses are simply paid for with cash (this is why a daily income and expense log is so helpful).

Separate your expenses into three categories: savings and investments, fixed expenses and variable expenses.

1. **Savings and Investments.** Savings and investments should include all monies periodically set aside in

   - bank accounts and products (e.g., certificates of deposit—CDs);
   - cans, jars and piggy banks;
   - club savings plans (e.g., Christmas club);
   - credit unions;
   - employer retirement savings plans (e.g., 401(k) plans);
   - individual retirement accounts (IRAs);
   - investment products (e.g., stock);
   - Keogh plans;
   - money market mutual funds and deposit accounts;
   - tax-sheltered annuities; and
   - thrift plans.

2. **Fixed Expenses.** Fixed expenses remain constant for at least six months to a year before changing, if they

change at all. Often, little can be done to reduce or control them. For example, payments on a fixed-rate mortgage are set according to amortization tables and are adjusted perhaps once a year according to the escrow needed for property taxes and insurance. Certain utility costs and insurance premiums are also set in advance by the provider. Although most fixed expenses eventually change, they are generally easier to forecast in the short term. Some examples of fixed expenses are

- budget plan utility payments (e.g., fuel oil);
- installment debt;
- insurance premiums;
- loan payments;
- mortgage;
- planned payroll deductions (e.g., group insurance);
- rent; and
- utilities with fixed periodic payments (e.g., sewage)

3. **Variable Expenses.** Conversely, variables change from month to month. They are easier to control and adjust in a spending plan but more difficult to predict. Some examples of variable expenses are

- alcohol and tobacco products;
- allowances and other money given to children;
- books, records and tapes;
- business expenses;
- charitable contributions;
- child care;
- clothing and clothing care (e.g., dry cleaning);

- educational expenses (e.g., tuition and books);
- entertainment (e.g., movies, theater, parties);
- fees and dues (e.g., union);
- food;
- garbage removal;
- gifts;
- health club memberships;
- hobbies (e.g., stamp collection);
- home and car maintenance;
- home furnishings and appliances;
- home improvements;
- meals eaten at restaurants;
- medical and dental expenses;
- miscellaneous expenses;
- parental support;
- personal care (e.g., haircuts, cosmetics);
- pet care (e.g., veterinarian);
- postage;
- professional fees (e.g., lawyer);
- recreation (e.g., bowling, golf);
- subscriptions to newspapers and magazines;
- taxes (e.g., Social Security);
- transportation, tolls and parking;
- utilities lacking fixed monthly payments (e.g., telephone); and
- vacations.

Again, you will need to refer to your checkbook, paycheck stubs and tax returns, as well as copies of recently paid bills, loan coupon books, expense account records, credit card statements and cash register receipts. All of these will help you reconstruct your spending and serve as reminders of expenses incurred. Also, be sure to include funds set aside in a savings account or in envelopes as part of an informal budget plan for large upcoming expenses (e.g., car insurance). Any outlay, by cash, check or credit, must be recorded, no matter how small.

The miscellaneous expenses section of the variable expense listing should total no more than about $200. Otherwise, it will be difficult to identify exact causes of overspending. As much as possible, every expense should be identified with a heading. The heading, however, is not as important as the recognition of how much you spend.

When you've tallied your expenses, subtract the total from your income. Is the result a positive number? If so, congratulations! You're in a good position to put money aside for future goals because a cash surplus remains at the end of the month.

If your cash flow is negative, don't despair. You'll simply need to work harder. Start by scrutinizing the expense section of your cash flow statement. Circle the expenses that will soon cease (e.g., a car loan about to be paid off) and those that you feel could be pared down. Could you spend less on food, clothing, restaurant meals and utilities such as your phone bill? That $2.50 a day spent on coffee, a roll and newspapers adds up to more than $900 a year! Until you become aware of your spending habits, it's hard to make realistic estimates for the future or find the dollars available to save.

In Chapter 6, you will find a list of 60 ways to live on less. It's important to make expense reductions with a positive attitude, however, or you'll feel like you're depriving yourself. Concentrate on your financial goals

Figure 4.1   The X. Ample Family

Cash Flow for the Year Ending December 31, 1993

Cash balance at beginning of year (1)	$250
Income	
Salaries after taxes (2)	$24,725
Inheritance	5,000
Tax refund	2,015
Interest	850
Lottery prize	500
Gifts	400
Christmas bonus	300
Dividends	140
	$33,930
Total Income	$34,180
Expenses	
Savings and Investments (3)	$6,500
Fixed Expenses	
Mortgage payments (4)	$6,744
Car loan payments (5)	2,268
Insurance premiums (6)	2,163
Fuel oil budget plan (7)	1,440
	$12,615

Figure 4.1 The X. Ample Family (Continued)

Variable Expenses	
Food	$5,160
Utilities (8)	1,610
Transportation	1,280
Clothing and clothing care	1,700
Vacation	800
Gifts	600
Medical and dental care	430
Recreation	400
Home furnishings	400
Children's allowance	385
Charitable contributions	250
Personal care	220
Subscriptions	210
Miscellaneous expenses	200
	$13,645
Total Expenses	$32,760
Cash balance at end of year	$1,420

Footnotes
(1) Cash and checking account balance
(2) FICA, federal and state income taxes totaled $7,185
(3) $1,500, money market; $1,000, Christmas club; $4,000, IRAs
(4) $562 monthly payment includes property taxes and insurance
(5) Monthly payment of $189
(6) Auto, $800; life, $653; disability, $585; umbrella, $125
(7) Twelve monthly payments of $120
(8) Electricity, telephone, water, sewer and garbage removal

Figure 4.2 Cash Flow Statement

Cash Flow for the Period _____ **(month, year)**
   List below the type and the amount of household income and expenses for a given time period (month, quarter, year, etc.).

Cash balance at the beginning of _____ (period): $ _____

Income
(e.g., salaries, interest, gifts, refunds, cash awards and prizes)

_____
_____
_____
_____
_____
_____

Total Income $ _____

Expenses

Savings and Investments
(e.g., IRAs, savings accounts, Christmas clubs, retirement savings plans) $_____

Fixed Expenses
(e.g., mortgage, car loan, installment debt, rent, insurance premiums)

_____
_____
_____
_____

Figure 4.2   Cash Flow Statement (Continued)

_____

_____

Variable Expenses
(e.g., clothing, food, gifts, pet care, entertainment, vacations)

_____

_____

_____

_____

_____

_____

_____

_____

_____

_____

Total Expenses $ _____

Cash balance at the end of _____ (period): $ _____

Footnotes

_____

_____

_____

_____

and how great you'll feel when you achieve them. In
Figure 4.1, you will find a sample cash flow statement
and, in Figure 4.2, a blank form totally your own income
and expenses.

How Much Do Others Earn and Spend?

If you've ever wondered how much it costs an average
family to live an average American lifestyle and how
much we spend on various expenses, you are not alone.
Creditors, college financial aid officers and government
policymakers (among others) share your interest.

The federal government collects household expense
data through ongoing consumer expenditure surveys
(CES) conducted by the Bureau of Labor Statistics of the
U.S. Department of Labor. Data are collected in two
independent parts: a quarterly interview and a diary survey covering two consecutive weeks. Each survey
includes about 5,000 households and is collected in 85
urban areas. CES data are the primary government
source of information about household spending.

Not surprisingly, CES data show that higher income
households spend more for food and housing than lower
income households but, as a percentage of total expenditures, the amount spent is proportionately lower. Food
and housing also compose a smaller proportional
demand on income in two-earner households than in
one-earner households.

Naturally, no hard and fast rules exist. Personal goals
and values differ and a home in Manhattan, New York,

could cost five times that of one in Manhattan, Kansas. Listed below are the percentages of after-tax income that average U.S. households allocated to various expense categories in 1990:

Housing	31%
Food	15%
Clothing	6%
Health care	5%
Entertainment	5%
Vehicles and Transportation	18%
Pensions and Life Insurance	9%
Other	11%

Again, there is no ideal way to spend money and personal circumstances vary tremendously. A couple in their fifties with a paid-up mortgage and a $40,000-a-year income might spend on housing a quarter of what two similarly paid twentysomethings spend on housing. If one or more of your expense categories seem far out of line, however, they may signal necessary readjustments. Reducing the amount of any expense category will provide additional cash for saving.

10 Ways To Achieve (and Maintain) Positive Cash Flow

① **Organize Your Records**—Designate a "money space" as the official depository for all financial records.

The exact location is up to you (desk, kitchen cabinet, etc.). Invest in some file folders and set up a filing system that works. Suggested categories include tax deduction receipts, current bills and recent canceled checks. Track your income and expenses at least once a year to determine whether adjustments to cash flow are necessary. It is also a good idea for both spouses in a married-couple household to handle the recordkeeping (together or alternately) so that both have firsthand knowledge of income and expense figures.

②   **Carry Less Cash and Plastic**—Impulse buying is more difficult if you don't routinely carry your checkbook and credit cards (you'll also have less to report if your wallet or purse is lost or stolen). Carrying less cash and refraining from the use of automatic teller machines for withdrawals will also help keep expenses down. Checks should be written for specific expenses instead of to "cash."

③   **Give Everyone an Allowance**—To avoid being "nickeled and dimed," give everyone in the household (adults and children) an allowance to spend as he or she pleases. The allowance should be realistic and firm. Giving a child a $15-a-week allowance instead of $25 here and there can reduce household expenses by more than $500 a year. An allowance also teaches money management skills and gives the recipient some spending flexibility.

④   **Earmark a Raise**—If you receive a raise, ignore it and continue to live on the salary you were earning before. Use the extra money in your paycheck to increase savings or reduce debt. Either way, you'll improve your standard of living.

⑤ **Use Equal Payment Plans**—Utility bills can vary sharply from season to season, making it difficult to know what to expect. Equal payment plans take the guesswork out of bill paying and even out household cash flow. Summer is traditionally the time when utilities (gas and electric companies and fuel oil merchants) begin plans for the following heating season. These plans usually run for 10-month or 12-month periods. With most plans, the total annual bill is calculated, based on actual energy use for the preceding year. It's then divided into equal monthly payments. For example, if a home costs $1,800 annually to heat, a 12-month budget plan would assess $150 monthly. The homeowner knows in advance exactly what the payment will be instead of being surprised with a $400 bill sometime during the winter.

⑥ **Increase Your Income**—Cash flow can be improved by increasing income as well as by reducing expenses. Some ways to increase your income include adding a spouse to the labor force, performing free-lance consulting work, turning a hobby into a business, moonlighting at a second job, watching other people's children for pay and helping your teenage children find part-time employment.

⑦ **Refinance Your Mortgage**—If the interest rate on your mortgage is a percent or more over current rates and you plan to remain in your home long enough to recoup closing costs, it may pay to take out a new mortgage. The advantages of refinancing include reducing monthly payments when interest rates decline, assessing home equity and consolidating high-interest debt. To determine whether refinancing is cost-effective, divide the estimated closing costs by the amount of monthly savings multiplied by 1 minus your marginal tax bracket. For example, if a no-points loan costs $1,500 to close and saves $104 per month, the after-tax savings is $75 ($104 times .72) for a homeowner in the 28 percent marginal tax bracket. Dividing $1,500 by $75 yields a breakeven period of 20 months.

⑧ **Withhold Taxes Correctly**—Instead of receiving a large tax refund each spring, you could put the money to work now. Proper withholding is the key. A $2,000 income tax refund is equivalent to having about $165 a month of additional income available for saving or spending.

⑨ **Don't Keep Secrets**—"His" and "Her" accounts can be a source of difficulty if spouses don't communicate about financial matters. In order to track cash flow accurately, *all* income and expenses must be accounted for.

⑩ **Build In Rewards**—Tracking cash flow and reducing monthly expenses take discipline. Reward yourself periodically with small but meaningful incentives (e.g., dinner at a restaurant), which can be anticipated in advance as variable expenses in a spending plan.

Like a net worth statement, a cash flow analysis provides no guarantee of wealth. It simply makes you aware of how you spend your money. A cash flow statement is, however, an essential prerequisite to a spending plan. Without it, you'll be flying blind, unable to make realistic estimates of future income and expenses.

5

Stash Some Cash—25 Ways
To Save More Money

Saving money is a lot like those weight loss programs frequently touted on television by celebrities. It's hard to get started, it's even harder to remain motivated, it requires a lot of patience and discipline but the results can be spectacular and make you feel great.

But you don't have a cent to spare? Nonsense. Saving money is a matter of priorities and attitude. You just have to want it badly enough. Think about this for a minute: If a parent or child were gravely ill, would you postpone visiting or caring for that person until you could "someday" come up with the money for a plane ticket or doctor's bills? Of course not. You'd be there for your loved one because his or her welfare is important to you. Somehow you'd find the money.

Somehow you must also find the savings dollars necessary to secure your financial future, even on a shoestring budget. The best way to start is to pick one or more savings methods, such as a Christmas club or an employer thrift plan, that work for you. The more automatic the savings method, the better. Many people eliminate the temptation to spend their savings by never seeing the money in the first place. Below is a list of 25 savings methods that work.

① **Pay Yourself First**—Treat savings like any other household bill. Put a part of each paycheck, even if it is only a few dollars, into savings and leave it there. If necessary, "bill" yourself, or remind yourself of the need to save, with post-it-notes or have a spouse or another trusted person deposit your savings for you before you can spend the money. Charge yourself interest, if savings are withdrawn, to replenish your account balance.

② **Collect Coins**—Put all loose change into a can or jar. As the container fills, deposit the money into a savings account. If you can save a dollar a day, plus all your pocket change, you should have about $50 a month, or $600 a year, set aside. Saving $2 a day, plus all your pocket change, should yield a nest egg of about $80 a month, or $1,000 a year (with interest). Get in the habit of making change to increase your level of savings. If the daily newspaper costs 35 cents, give the clerk a dollar and save the 65 cents you get back. Also, be sure to inquire about your bank's policy on handling loose change. Some institutions ask that you deposit coins rolled in special wrappers while others prefer that you bring coins to the bank unwrapped so that they can be counted by machine. Figure 5.1 illustrate how savings can add up over time.

③ **Bank Your Refunds**—When you receive a refund for the purchase of a product in the supermarket or a manufacturer's rebate (used today for everything from videotapes to appliances to automobiles), save it. Track your refund and rebate income so you know how much you've earned in a year. Refunding proceeds are considered nontaxable income by the Internal Revenue Service (IRS) unless (and this is highly unlikely) rebates exceed the cost of the items that were purchased to quality for them. Some states also rebate a portion of qualifying residents' property taxes. This money, too, can be set aside for future goals.

④ **Continue Paying Off a Loan**—Have you just finished (or are you about to finish) paying for furniture or a car? Continue making the same monthly payment—to yourself! The rationale behind this savings method is that you are already accustomed to the monthly loan payment. Assuming that a new loan is not needed immediately, placing the monthly payment in your savings account should be relatively painless, with little or no effect on your lifestyle. Let's assume that you're just about to pay off a $190-a-month, 48-month car loan and that you expect your car to last another three years (seven years total—about average for today's car). By placing the $190 a month in a savings product averaging 7 percent, you'd have almost $7,500 when it's time to buy your next car.

⑤ **Break Costly Habits**—Do you really need to buy breakfast or lunch out every day? Are you trying to stop smoking? Saving the money that you would normally spend on habits like these might just improve your health as well as your wealth. The results are not insignificant, either. A $7-a-day habit of eating at work, for example, costs $1,750 over the course of a year (this calculation even assumes that you take a two-week vaca-

Figure 5.1   How Regular Savings Can Build a Small Fortune

Time Horizon	Annual Investment			
	$500	$1,000	$5,000	$10,000
5 years	$ 2,930	$ 5,865	$ 29,330	$ 58,665
10 years	7,240	14,485	72,430	144,865
20 years	22,880	45,760	228,810	457,620
30 years	56,640	113,280	566,415	1,132,830

Assumes an 8 percent return compounded annually, before taxes.

tion). If you brown-bag-it just two days a week, you'll cut this expense by $600. Depending on the extent of your smoking habit, quitting can save $500 to $2,500 in a year, or $5,000 to $25,000 in a decade.

⑥   **Increase Investment Yields**—Don't settle for low interest rates! Earn more money on the money you've already saved by seeking investments, consistent with your risk tolerance level, that pay a higher rate of return. One of the lowest yielding savings vehicles today is the passbook savings account. Because most pay less than a 4 percent interest rate, you'd think that they'd be shunned by consumers. Quite the contrary. In 1990, more than $418 billion sat in passbook savings accounts. Yet, at their favorite local bank, depositors could easily have earned a higher return by transferring their money to a CD, Treasury bill or U.S. savings bond. When shopping for a savings account, avoid products with high fees or service charges and maximize your return with accounts that compound interest frequently.

⑦ **Join a Credit Union**—Credit unions are a convenient way to save and a relatively inexpensive source of funds when you need a loan. Deposits can be automatically deducted from your paycheck, which increases the probability that part of your earnings will be saved. Limited hours of operation (many credit unions are open only on weekdays during business hours—the same hours that most people work) also increase the chance that your money will stay put. Credit unions are generally available only to groups of people with a similar affiliation or common bond. Approximately three-quarters of more than 60 million credit union customers become members through their employers, with the remainder joining credit unions that serve a particular residential area, professional association or trade union. In recent years, many credit unions have increased their product lines to include credit and debit cards, CDs, home equity loans and guaranteed student loans in addition to their traditional share-draft (checking) accounts.

⑧ **Buy U.S. Savings Bonds**—For as little as $25, you can buy a U.S. savings bonds that will eventually double in value (e.g., $25 to $50). Savings bonds held at least five years pay an average of semi-annually adjusted market-based rates (4.25 percent in early 1994). Bonds redeemed before five years earn the guaranteed minimum rate of 4 percent. Series EE bonds are sold in denominations of $50, $100, $200, $500, $1,000, $5,000 and $10,000. The bonds are redeemable at face value when they mature. Series HH bonds make interest payments every six months and can be purchased in denominations of $500 to $10,000 in exchange for EE bonds.

Both HH bonds and EE bonds can be redeemed at any time, starting six months after the date they are issued. Series EE bonds can be purchased at most commercial banks and at many savings and loans. Some employers also have U.S. savings bond plans for their employees, where payroll deductions are used to purchase bonds on a periodic basis. For information about the latest market-based rates on U.S. savings bonds, call 1-800-USBONDS.

⑨ **Take Advantage of Direct Deposit**—If your employer has an arrangement with local banks to deposit employee paychecks electronically, consider signing up for it. Your paycheck will be deposited automatically in your checking or savings account each payday, saving you the time spent driving to a bank and waiting in line to cash your paycheck. If you're concerned that you'll miss having the actual check in your hand, don't be. Most employers that offer a direct deposit service also provide employees with a receipt or a paycheck stub that indicates their current salary, payroll deductions and year-to-date totals. Once your paycheck is deposited in a bank, you must then, of course, resolve to keep some of it there. For some people, this savings method works because it is harder, psychologically, to make withdrawals than deposits. Automatic payroll deposit has become increasingly popular since electronic fund transfers were made possible by computer technology in the 1970s.

⑩ **Participate in an Employer's Thrift Plan**—Thrift plans are an after-tax dollar savings program to which employees make voluntary contributions through payroll deduction. In addition to automatically saving a portion of employees' pay, some employers match thrift plan contributions by 25 cents or 50 cents (or more) on the dollar. The match may be based on factors such as years of service or the amount of an employee's contribution or both. Often, employees are given a choice of thrift plan investments (bond fund, stock fund, money market fund, etc.). Employers usually prescribe minimum and maximum savings amounts (usually a percentage of an employee's salary) and make policies concerning the suspension of thrift plan contributions, changes in savings rates and withdrawals from the plan.

⑪ **Have Uncle Sam Save for You**—IRS studies show that about three-quarters of all taxpayers receive refunds and that average refund amounts during 1991–92 were just less than $1,000. While getting a check each spring sounds great, people who have their income tax overwithheld are actually lending money interest free to the government. Another drawback of having income tax overwithheld is that you have to wait for "your" money. Excess payments are not readily available and you must file a tax form and wait for a refund. Even though tax overwithholding is not the best savings method available, it is, nevertheless, one method people use to save money. If you decide to join them, start by correctly filling out a W-4 form. Ideally, you and Uncle Sam should come out about even. Then you can adjust your withholding according to the amount that you want to save. The beginning of a new tax year is the best time to check your W-4 because your withholding will be accurate from the start. By having your employer withhold too much, you take home a smaller paycheck. If too little is withheld, you will owe a large tax bill and, perhaps, penalties. If two wage earners live in a household, the most accurate approach is to claim all eligible allowances on the higher paying job and to claim zero allowances on the other. Also, be sure to adjust your tax withholding when major financial changes occur. A first or trade-up house, for example, generally brings with it higher tax deductions than taken previously. Both the interest on the new mortgage and property taxes are deductible under current tax law. In the 15, 28 and 31 percent marginal tax brackets, the tax savings on a $10,000 real estate deduction (interest and property taxes combined) is $1,500, $2,800 and $3,100, respectively. A death, divorce, birth of a child and large capital gain or loss are other events with major tax implications.

⑫ **Start a Christmas or Vacation Club**—While money deposited in these accounts usually does not earn a high rate of interest, savings do accumulate in small amounts, enabling people to reach future goals. The small weekly payment won't be missed and provides a sizeable check later on. Club plans can generally be started at a bank in weekly amounts as low as $2 to $5, with maximums ranging up to $50 or $100. The interest earned is comparable to that of a passbook savings account. The funds can, of course, be used for *any* purpose. People who have short-term financial goals that coincide with the times that distributions are made might consider using club plans as a savings method. For many, the psychological reinforcement of having a teller remove each coupon and stamp the weekly club coupon book provides just the incentive that is needed to save.

Club participants also know exactly how much they'll have at the end of the savings period. Fifty $20 weekly payments will provide $1,000 plus interest a year later. You can accumulate $2,000 for each year's maximum IRA contribution by starting a $40-a-week Christmas club. A final advantage of club savings plans is that some banks give savers a gift of some sort at the start of each year's savings program. That same $2,000-a-year IRA could be funded with four $10-a-week clubs or eight $5-a-week clubs if a saver desired more free gifts and didn't mind carrying around the extra coupon books. If you can't be bothered opening another bank account, borrow the Christmas club philosophy and save the extra dollars each week on your own.

⑬ **Bank a Windfall**—A windfall, quite simply, is a large sum of money, often unexpected, received on a one-time or limited basis. Whenever you receive a windfall, such as an inheritance, bingo or raffle winnings, retroactive pay, an award, an insurance dividend or a year-end-bonus, put at least part of the money into savings. The thinking behind this advice is that the money was not anticipated and is therefore not part of your normal household cash flow. If you hadn't received the windfall, you would have managed without it. A common windfall is a lump-sum pension or retirement plan distribution received when employees change jobs. Suddenly, they are given responsibility for a large sum of cash, perhaps tens of thousands of dollars, and forced to make a quick decision about handling these funds. One recent study found that only about 4 percent of employees who receive a lump-sum pension distribution roll it over into an IRA or another tax-deferred retirement plan and 10 percent use the money to buy a house. About 63 percent, the vast majority, squander the distribution on disposable items such as cars, clothing and vacations. This is a mistake. The money should be saved or invested for retirement, with professional advice strongly suggested to answer tax and investment-related questions. More suggestions for handling windfalls are included at the end of this chapter.

⑭ **Crash Save**—The keys to successfully using this savings strategy are a relatively inexpensive goal and a limited time frame. Decide that for, say, two months you'll buy only absolute necessities and save any money remaining. At the end of the two months, treat yourself and buy the item(s) you were saving for. Then resume your normal spending habits or set a new goal. Let's say your children want a $300 VCR in ten weeks for Christmas. By crash saving $30 a week, the funds will be there. This savings method works especially well for children because the payoff for setting aside money is visible after only a short time. The euphoric feeling of being able to purchase something you want is a powerful motivator to save money again in the future. Many people never go back to their normal routine again because saving becomes part of their lifestyle.

⑮ **Fund IRAs One Week at a Time**—Between 1986 and 1987, IRA contributions fell by 62 percent after tax law changes limited their deductibility. By 1992, just more than 4 million tax returns reported IRA deductions, down from 15 million in 1986. Nevertheless, all workers younger than age 70^1/$_2$ with earned income may contribute up to $2,000 to an IRA. To avoid having to come up with a large sum all at once, try to set aside about $40 each week. As you accumulate the amount of money needed for a minimum deposit (e.g., $100, $250 or $500), place it in an IRA. At the end of the year, you'll have saved $2,000 (plus earnings on the IRA). Use this same strategy for a Keogh plan if you're self-employed. As the tax year progresses, you'll have a better idea of your expected net business earnings and the maximum contribution you're allowed.

⑯　**Participate in a 401(k) Plan**—If you're a corporate employee and your employer offers a 401(k) plan, you can reduce your salary (by payroll deduction) to save for retirement. Better still, if your employer matches your contribution (typically 50 cents on the dollar), every $1 invested automatically becomes $1.50. Both the money contributed to a 401(k) plan and the earnings on these funds grow tax deferred until withdrawal. The maximum amount of pay that can be contributed to a 401(k) account increased from $7,000 in 1987 to $9,240 in 1994 and will increase again in future years. The limit is based on a formula that adjusts the cap yearly to reflect rises in the cost of living. Like the thrift plans discussed earlier, 401(k)s generally offer participants a choice of investment options.

⑰　**Participate in a 403(b) Plan**—If you're a teacher, college professor or nonprofit organization employee and your employer offers such a plan, you can reduce your salary by up to $9,500 a year for retirement savings. Like the 401(k) plan, the 403(b) is a before-tax dollar savings plan and generally offers a choice of investment options. A major difference between the two plans is that nonprofit sector employers generally don't match 403(b) employee contributions. 403(b) plans also offer a special catch-up provision for persons who don't begin participating until late in their careers. The exact amount is based on salary and length of service.

⑱ **Participate in a Government Employees' Retirement Savings Plan**—A third type of before-tax dollar retirement savings plan exists for county and municipal government employees. It's called a Section 457 deferred compensation plan and allows annual contributions of up to $7,500. Like those of 403(b)s, the contributions generally are not matched by employers. Many financial experts advise investing as much money as you can afford in any type of salary-reduction plan (401(k), 403(b) or Section 457) *before* contributing money to an IRA, particularly a nondeductible one (more about this in Chapter 12). This is because both the contribution you make by reducing your salary and the plan's earnings are tax deferred regardless of income. A second advantage is that employers do the saving for you. If you can afford it, you can have both a salary reduction plan and an IRA. It is a good idea to calculate your maximum exclusion allowance annually for any type of salary-reduction plan to make sure that you don't exceed the maximum amount you're allowed by law to contribute.

⑲ **Save Your "Extra" Paychecks**—If you're paid biweekly, in two months of the year you will receive

Figure 5.2 Anticipating "Extra" Paychecks

Sunday	Monday	Tuesday	Wednesday	Thursday	Friday	Saturday
			1	2	3	4
5	6	7	8	9	10	11
12	13	14	15	16	17	18
19	20	21	22	23	24	25
26	27	28	29	30	31	

three paychecks. Employees who are paid weekly will receive an "extra" check in four months of each year. The months vary according to each year's calendar and the day of the week on which you are paid. In Figure 5.2, for example, an employee receiving a weekly paycheck on either Wednesday, Thursday or Friday would receive five paychecks in the month illustrated. Workers paid biweekly, starting with the first week of the month, would receive three checks if paid on those same days. The key to using this method of saving is to anticipate the months with extra paychecks in advance and divert all or part of the additional pay into savings. After all, during the other months of the year, you got along on one fewer paycheck.

⑳ **Save Excess Expense Account Reimbursement Money**—Many employees who are required to travel as part of their job are reimbursed 18 to 29 cents per mile for business-related mileage. With an older car that's fully depreciated, the amount you're reimbursed can exceed by two to five times the actual cost of gasoline, oil and repairs (depending on your car and the amount of driving you do). Place this excess money in a separate savings account and use it for future car purchases and auto maintenance costs. *Don't* spend this money on general household expenses unless absolutely necessary. You also can use expense account funds to pay miscellaneous business expenses, union or professional association dues, conference registration fees and other expenses related to your occupation. The money adds up over time (e.g., $50 a month excess times 12 months equals $600) and helps you avoid having to tap general household funds to cover job-related expenses.

㉑   **Borrow To Save**—Some people actually do well by borrowing their savings from a bank and paying themselves back. The structure of a loan provides the needed incentive to save. This strategy should be used *only* when the interest earned on savings is greater than or equal to the after-tax cost of the loan. Also, a saver must have the discipline not to spend the borrowed funds until the loan is repaid. With the interest deduction on consumer loans completely phased out since 1992, this strategy is more difficult to use than in the past. Nevertheless, it can work occasionally. If a saver in the 28 percent marginal tax bracket takes out a tax-deductible home equity loan with interest costs averaging 9 percent, the after-tax cost of borrowing is 6.48 percent. If the saver could earn this amount or more on a savings or an investment product, it would be cost-efficient to borrow his or her savings. Unfortunately, it is difficult to know the average cost of a home equity loan over a number of years because many loans have variable rates pegged to a market rate index. Repaying the loan as quickly as possible will reduce this risk of uncertainty.

㉒ **Reinvest Interest and Dividends Automatically**—When you purchase any type of savings or investment product, arrange to have the interest or dividends reinvested rather than taking the money out and spending it. Automatic reinvestment plans are a convenient and painless way to increase personal savings and, over the long term, the results can be spectacular! Consider a growth mutual fund in which $10,000 is invested for 20 years (1968 to 1988) and earns the equivalent of the Standard & Poor's 500 Stock Index. If the dividends were taken in cash and not reinvested, the value of the investment in 1988 would be about $37,200: the original $10,000 investment plus an increase of almost $16,500 in principal value plus about $10,700 received in cash dividends. If the dividends were reinvested, however, the value of the portfolio would be almost $61,300, or about 60 percent more. The value of the reinvested dividends alone would be $34,800, a great return for just leaving your money alone!

㉓ **Keep Checking Account Balances to a Minimum**—Many people make the mistake of keeping large balances in a non-interest-bearing checking account. Over time, this costs them a lot of money. Ideally, your checking account balance should be just slightly larger than your monthly expenses. If you build up a surplus, transfer the excess funds to an interest-bearing savings or investment product. An interest-bearing NOW or SuperNOW checking account is another option if you can keep a balance large enough to avoid penalties and service charges.

㉔   **Take Advantage of Float**—The word *float* is used in the banking industry to describe situations where the presenter of a check is granted the use of funds until the check has cleared. Subtraction of the face amount of the check from the account balance has yet to take place. With interest-bearing accounts, such as a money market fund or money market deposit account with check-writing privileges, it is advantageous to extend the float period in order to continue earning interest on your money. One way to save before a check is even written is to pay bills a few days, instead of a few weeks, ahead of their due date. This will keep your money in your account for as long as possible without penalty. Also, avoid using debit cards or computerized bill-paying arrangements, which deduct bills immediately from your account. Neither of these systems of payment offers float.

㉕   **Pay Off Debt**—Would you like to earn 17 to 21 percent on your money? Pay off your credit cards! If you carry an average account balance of, say, $600, you probably pay about $100 to $130 in interest a year. Paying off this debt is equivalent to earning the amount of interest charged by your creditor. Because most credit cards charge four to five times the interest rate paid to savers on passbook accounts, paying off previously accumulated debt is one of the smartest investments you can make. Yet, surprisingly, fewer people are doing so. Less than 30 percent of credit card holders today pay their balance in full, compared to about half five years ago. Another cost-saving strategy is to seek a lower interest credit card if you habitually carry over a monthly balance. For a list of banks that issue such cards, contact Bankcard Holders of America, 6862 Elm Street, #300, McLean, VA 22101 or call 703-389-5445. For a nominal charge, they will send you a list of credit cards with low rates.

How To Handle a Windfall

Someday, you might—just might—receive a large cash windfall. Sometimes it is earned, as in the case of a lump-sum pension distribution, and sometimes it is unearned, such as a court settlement, an inheritance or gambling proceeds. A large windfall can create as much trouble as a drop in income if not handled properly. Even if you make it big, the odds are against your keeping the money. Taxes and inflation are the enemies of anyone trying to preserve a nest egg.

Let's suppose you win $1 million in the state lottery. Congratulations! You will probably receive $50,000 per year for 20 years. That's very different from getting $1 million in a lump sum and Uncle Sam will probably take a third right off the top. No problem, you say. That still leaves you with about $34,000 per year for 20 years, right? Wrong! Inflation will cut your purchasing power over time and your lottery checks in future years will be worth much less in today's dollars. Surprised? You shouldn't be. Inflation, no matter what the rate, is a fact of life.

So what should you do to hold on to a windfall, should you receive one? Below are five tips to consider.

① **Remember that one-shot windfalls, like an inheritance, cannot be replaced.** Therefore, treat this money more conservatively than you would a permanent increase in earnings. If you plan to use a windfall to buy a better home, for example, make a sizeable down payment so that your mortgage will be no larger than it is currently. If you want to supplement your income, invest the windfall and spend only the interest.

② **Diversify your windfall** on the premise that risks in some investments will be offset by relative safety factors in others.

③ **Plan for inflation.** Let's assume it will be 4 percent for the next few years. Your investments will have to earn an after-tax return of at least that amount in order to maintain purchasing power. Anything less and it's rags to riches to rags.

④ **If your windfall is a lump-sum pension distribution, arrange for an IRA rollover.** Otherwise, this money, which has been growing tax deferred, will be subject to federal income tax and, perhaps, a 10 percent penalty.

⑤ **Be sensible.** Don't try to reduce taxes at all costs. Look at the investment aspects of a financial product first; then judge the merits of the tax savings.

Remember, a windfall provides a priceless advantage: a chunk of capital to invest for the future. Don't spend it

without a well-designed plan. Following the above tips
will help keep your assets intact.

Well, What Are You Waiting For?

It is important to remember that financial planning
doesn't just happen. Someone, you or a professional
adviser, must initiate the process and ultimately you
must live with the results. Lack of financial planning is
also a type of plan, one that is designed by default. If you
don't prepare a will, the state where you reside will dis-
tribute your assets for you. If you don't plan your taxes,
you could overpay Uncle Sam a small fortune.

Planning alone is not enough. Many people make
elaborate plans but fail to carry them out. To avoid this
common error, start with a list of have-to's—that is,
actions you must take to achieve your financial goals.
Then immediately make some changes, starting with
increasing your monthly savings.

A law of physics states: a body at rest remains at rest
and a body in motion remains in motion. Some people
remain at rest and never get started on the road to financial success. They use excuses such as "As soon as my
kids are out of college, I'll start saving" or "As soon as I
pay off the car loan, I'll start planning for my retirement." Years later, their plans remain unachieved because
they're still waiting for something to change.

Why is it that so many people fail to achieve their
goals while others turn their dreams into reality? Very
simply, successful people plan ahead and develop and
maintain a positive mental attitude. They think about

their goals and reject thoughts of failure. They see obstacles as challenges and take charge of their lives instead of waiting for things to happen. They plan for decades instead of for the weekend. Think about it: perception is reality! When you think and act positively, you'll achieve the best for yourself and your family.

6

Spend Less, Save More—
60 Ways To Cut Expenses

*You're looking at a coat. The price is marked down
and you're debating whether to buy it. How about that
color TV? It's 25 percent off the regular price today. A
Porsche sure would be nice, too. Your credit card company says go for it.*

We have all been there, hundreds of times: the consumer spending crossroads. All too often, when we
decide to buy something, we get a nagging feeling that
we could spend the money in a better way. It's usually
vague and subconscious but it can spoil the pleasure we
might otherwise get from a product or service. Worse
yet, the purchase leaves us without the money we had,
money that could have been used for wiser purchases or
for savings and investments.

So how do we avoid the habit—and it is a habit—of
wasteful spending? One solution is to approach spending
positively rather than taking the negative and often futile
approach of trying to break a bad habit (just ask any
smoker or dieter who has tried to reform). The National

Center for Financial Education (NCFE) in San Diego calls this concept "spending by choice" and it works something like this: Instead of saying to yourself, "Should I buy this?" you say "This is the amount of money I am going to earmark this month (or this paycheck) for spending. Am I sure this is how I want to spend it?" In other words, you ask yourself how you want to spend your money instead of telling yourself that you shouldn't spend it.

"I shouldn't spend this money" is what the NCFE calls negative input. Because it's negative, it's easy to ignore. That's how the human mind works. Negative input forces us to rationalize our purchases. "The color is good," "It's on sale" and "I really want it" are common examples. With spending by choice, your instinct to spend is still satisfied. It's like a dieter who cuts back on calories as long as he or she gets some ice cream every day. You're not trying to completely change your lifestyle and you don't have to overcome psychological resistance.

Don't make the mistake of thinking that spending by choice is simple. It's not. It requires a great deal of practice. Start by giving yourself some options, prioritizing them and making a shopping list (we make a list when we go to the supermarket—why not for our other purchases?). Ask yourself what else could be purchased, with the same amount of money, that you have needed or wanted for a long time. Compare at least three different merchants for price, service and quality. Do you see what's happened? *You* are in control. You'll buy what you really want, regardless of habit or impulse or guilt or advertising. If you form this habit, spend wisely and save the difference; you could be worth a fortune.

7 Common Spending Errors

Before you can develop the habit of spending by choice, you must understand how you handle money. People usually don't start saving without changing their spending habits. To save more, you'll need to spend less, unless you can increase your income. Start by examining the following seven spending errors

① **Buying on Impulse**—Are you an impulse buyer? If so, add up the cost of this habit. Purchasing $15 worth of impulse items each week costs $780 a year. Treat yourself every once in a while, of course, but try not to get carried away. If other people encourage you to spend more than you planned, try shopping alone.

② **Buying on Revolving Credit**—With interest rates on most credit cards ranging from 14 to 21 percent, credit is expensive! A $400 television financed at 15 percent over three years will cost $490, or almost 25 percent more than if purchased with cash. If you must shop with credit cards, pay off the outstanding balance as quickly as possible.

③ **Buying at the Wrong Time**—Buying clothing and seasonal merchandise (e.g., snow blowers and gas grills) at full price when they first arrive in a store is expensive. Before long, the price will be reduced, particularly in years when sales are slow. You also can save money by waiting for newly introduced products (e.g., calculators, computers and electronic equipment) to come down in price, by making phone calls at night and on weekends and by using store coupons.

④ **Buying Love or Power**—Some people make the mistake of equating love with spending money. Whenever they feel neglected or guilty about neglecting others, they make a major purchase to show that someone cares. Other people use money as a weapon or to cope with stress or depression. When they're angry at, say, a spouse, they head for the nearest mall to run up bills as punishment.

⑤ **Buying the "Wrong" Product**—You can save money by comparison shopping. If you're planning to buy an appliance, consult back issues of *Consumer Reports* for descriptions of available brands and models and performance ratings. Many department store brands are actually identical to name brands because they're made by the same manufacturer. Other money-saving items include store and generic food and household products, generic prescription drugs and energy-efficient appliances that will more than pay for themselves by reducing future utility costs.

⑥ **Buying Convenience**—Time-saving convenience foods are expensive. Single-serving packages of frozen name-brand lasagna, for example, can cost from 250 to 500 percent more than a similar-sized serving made from scratch. To save both time and money, bake or cook in batches and freeze the excess. Also, remember that convenience stores are expensive because their markups are higher than supermarkets' markups. The price differential between the two can total as much as $100 a year if convenience stores are used frequently. Another high-cost convenience item is the alternative operator service phone found in many hotel rooms. Bypass it completely by requesting to be connected to a major long-distance carrier.

⑦ **Buying Status**—Easy access to credit has made it easy to purchase goods and services on the spot. Some people get in over their heads when they develop a pattern of materialistic competition with friends or relatives. Money and possessions become equated, in their minds, with success. Status seekers try to buy bigger and better possessions than anyone else because they think that they can prove by the size of their home or the labels on their clothes that they're more successful.

60 Ways To Live on Less

Now that you've reviewed the seven major errors that cause people to waste their hard-earned money, let's talk specifics. Is it really possible to live on less and save the difference? Definitely. Many people do it every day. Sometimes cutbacks are planned and sometimes they are unexpected. Quitting a job to go to school, disability, a career change and unemployment are some common situations that may require a reduction in living expenses. Other situations include a two-paycheck family scaling back to live on one paycheck so that the other spouse can care for a young child, and persons who cut their expenses to increase their savings for future goals. Below are 60 relatively painless ways to cut living costs.

Food

1. Eliminate expensive convenience foods and prepared snacks fom your shopping list by making
   them yourself from scratch. Batch cook casseroles
   and main dishes for use at a later date.

2. Use nonfat dry milk in baking or combined (and
   chilled) with whole milk for drinking. Nonfat dry
   milk is cheaper than fresh milk and having it on
   hand will reduce emergency trips to the supermarket
   (buy and freeze an extra loaf of bread for this same
   reason).

3. Make a shopping list with prices itemized in
   advance and stick to it. Avoid impulse buying. Don't
   go to the supermarket unless absolutely necessary
   and try not to shop when you're hungry or with
   young children.

4. Search for bargains in the day-old bakery and dented-
   package bins. As long as cans are not bulging and
   leaking and other packages are unopened, it's safe to
   buy these foods if you use them immediately. Also,
   shop above or below eye level, where the less costly
   products on a shelf will be found.

5. Use cents-off coupons and refund forms but only on
   products you plan to buy anyway and only when the
   after-coupon cost is cheaper than alternative products. Send for free samples. In states with bottle
   bills, return containers that require a deposit.

6. When values are exceptional, buy another newspaper and revisit a supermarket, if it's convenient, with a second set of coupons. Another option is to give the second set of coupons to a spouse or child and split up when you go shopping.

7. Take advantage of double-coupon (and even triple-coupon) promotions. If they are not available where you live, they may be in the vicinity of friends and relatives. Take your coupons along whenever you travel.

8. Use lower cost store-brand or generic-brand products to save money at the supermarket. Store-brand products are often identical to nationally advertised brands and packed at the same processing plant.

9. Stock up on fresh fruits and vegetables when they are in season and can, freeze or dry them for use at a later date.

10. Read food advertisements weekly and stock up on products that are on sale. If a store is out of a particular advertised item, ask for a raincheck.

11. Cut up your own meat. The more preparation a store butcher does, the higher the cost of a package of meat. Cutting up your own chicken or stew beef could save up to $1 per pound and perhaps $200 a year.

12. Go where the bargains are. If there are several nearby supermarkets, choose the one(s) that has the best prices each week. Blind loyalty to any one store can be expensive.

13. Be a do-it-yourselfer (or get to know one). People who hunt, fish or grow their own fruits and vegetables have the advantage of a relatively inexpensive source of food.

14. Join a co-op that buys food in bulk. By trading off some time and labor, you may be able to purchase food less expensively than at a supermarket. Co-ops can also be found for babysitting and car pooling. They provide low-cost services to help members save money.

15. Read unit price labels and buy the least expensive size of a product based on cost per unit of weight. An exception, of course, are smaller households that don't need or want the large economy size.

16. Instead of going out to dinner with friends, plan a cooperative dinner party where each guest brings one course. You'll enjoy a fun evening with a minimum of preparation time and expense.

17. If you do go out to dinner and are frequently put in the position of having to split a check when your share is less than half, act quickly. Before the other parties offer to split the bill, figure out what you owe, including taxes and tip, and place the cash for your share on the table.

18. If you usually buy breakfast, snack foods or lunch at work or at a restaurant, "brown bag it" several days a week, especially if your employer provides a microwave oven.

19. Cook just the right amount of food for the size of your family. This will reduce waste and the possibility of leftovers ending up in the garbage because they remain in the refrigerator too long. Recipes should be multiplied or divided according to the needs of your household. Wrap food carefully and store it promptly to avoid spoilage.

20. Don't eat meat every night. It's expensive and most Americans consume more than enough protein. Instead, plan a variety of casseroles, soups, stews, egg dishes (e.g., quiche), poultry and seafood. In addition to cutting costs, you'll probably also reduce the fat and cholesterol content of your diet.

Clothing

21. Insist that family members not wear their good clothes for play or for working around the house, especially if the clothing must be dry cleaned. Use an apron when cooking.

22. Recycle clothing that can no longer be worn or take it to a consignment shop, which will sell it for you and split the profit. A third option is to have a garage sale or sell used clothing at a flea market.

23. Choose basic styles that can be dressed up or down and build your wardrobe around a few colors that compliment you.

24. Select new garments to go with clothing you already own. You should be able to get at least three outfits from each new item (five or more is even better).

25. Look for versatile garments that can be worn most of the year or year-round. Avoid novelty, high-fashion and faddish clothing, which will soon be out of style.

26. Buy quality, not quantity. Quality clothing lasts longer and looks better. The longer the expected life of a garment, the better the quality should be.

27. Shop at discount outlets and second-hand (consignment) stores. Discount stores sell quality and designer clothing at discounted prices by adding a smaller markup to wholesale prices than do department stores. Consignment stores sell unwanted clothing that is usually carefully screened for stains and flaws, with prices ranging from a quarter to half of the original price.

28. Visit a thrift shop. The quality is variable but the prices are generally lower than those of consignment stores and may be negotiable. Thrift shops are especially useful for garments needed for short-term wear, such as children's clothing, maternity wear and party clothes.

29. Follow fabric care labels and treat stains immediately. Failure to do so can permanently damage a garment. Fix rips and tears right away. Protect leather items from water and salt.

30. Dry clean clothing at a coin-operated dry cleaner or launder it by hand, when possible.

Utilities

31. Dry clothes in the house on clotheslines to save on charges at the Laundromat or on your utility bill. In the summer, dry clothing outdoors.

32. Write letters instead of making long-distance telephone calls, when possible, and use a timer to monitor the length of necessary telephone calls.

33. If long-distance telephone calls average $20 or more per month, try making these calls at night or on weekends and sign up for a long-distance package such as AT&T's "Reach Out America," MCI's "Friends and Family" or Sprint's "The Most." These programs allow you to make long-distance calls to specified people or at specified times at reduced rates.

34. Close off unused rooms to conserve heat. Fill in cracks around windows and doors. Caulk and weatherstrip doors and windows to save up to 10 percent on your energy bill. Pull down shades or draw draperies on cold winter nights to prevent heat loss or on hot days when the air-conditioning is on. Place at least six to nine inches of insulation in the attic.

35. Bake foods together as much as possible to save energy. Use a toaster oven or microwave, instead of a large oven, for warming leftovers or cooking for one or two people.

36. Contact your local utility company for an energy audit or to arrange for the installation of energy conservation measures. Some companies will send a contractor to your home and you'll be charged only for the materials used. Others provide rebates to encourage the purchase of energy-efficient appliances. Zero-interest loans may also be available for larger energy conservation projects.

37. Lower your thermostat by one degree and you'll save 1 to 2 percent on heating bills. Put on a sweater, keep your feet warm and buy an inexpensive humidifier, which will make your rooms feel warmer when the thermostat is turned down. Turn back the thermostat even more at night and when no one is home.

38. In the summer, use fans, instead of air conditioners, to cool your home.

39. Invest in no-cost or low-cost energy-saving activities such as an annual furnace tune-up, an insulation wrap on a water heater and a cleaning of the outside coils on a refrigerator once or twice a year. The biggest consumers of energy in a home are its heating system, hot water heater and refrigeration equipment. Anything that enhances the efficiency of these appliances, even a little, can provide significant savings.

40. If your utility offers a discount for electricity usage during off-peak hours (generally nights and weekends), sign up for it and buy a timer for your water heater so that it cycles on only during off-peak hours.

Miscellaneous Expenses

41. Don't buy insurance you don't need (e.g., life insurance on a child). If you have an adequate emergency fund, consider increasing deductibles, such as the collision deductible on car insurance and the elimination period on disability insurance. Also, take advantage of available discounts such as those given to nonsmokers or multicar households.

42. Don't buy products sold door to door and avoid in-home parties (e.g., copper, plasticware, crafts, etc.) where the temptation to spend is high. Set a cost limit or lid on gifts or make gifts from inexpensive materials. If you receive an expensive gift, don't feel that you must reciprocate with an item of equal monetary value.

43. If you must reorder checks for a checking account, don't buy them at your local bank. Banks charge markups as high as 100 percent on check printing and 200 plain checks can cost as much as $15. Instead, order your checks from a mail-order firm, which may charge from $4 to $6 for 200 personalized checks. Two of the largest firms are Current Inc. (P.O. Box 19000, Colorado Springs, CO 80935)

and Checks In The Mail (P.O. Box 7802, Irwindale, CA 91706). Both of these companies require a reorder form or voided check and deposit slip from your present check supply.

44. Cut your children's hair and cut or trim an adult's hair between professional cuttings.

45. Shop at discount outlets, thrift shops, garage sales, pawn shops and flea markets, and through newspaper classified ads, for gently used toys, appliances, jewelry, home furnishings and yard equipment. Another option is to swap or share these items with neighbors or family members.

46. Wash your own car and change your car's oil, oil filter and antifreeze. Take an auto repair course and learn how to do your own tune-ups and minor repairs.

47. Shop around for repairs and remodeling and home improvement work. Get several written estimates and a contract before hiring anyone to make major improvements to your home and check out contractors through a Better Business Bureau or state consumer affairs office.

48. Share a ride with others or take turns car pooling to work, school or community activities. If you routinely drive someone to work or school or if you take someone on a long trip, agree in advance on a reasonable reimbursement and collect it. Use self-service gas stations and those that offer a discount for

paying with cash. Consolidate errands that require driving.

49. Cut purchase, rental and subscription costs on books, records, videotapes and magazines by borrowing them at the public library. Subscribe to only those magazines and newspapers you have time to read and buy longer term subscriptions to reduce the cost per issue.

50. If you enjoy going to the theater or movies, attend lower cost matinees. Also, seek out free recreational activities. Use community resources such as health fairs, canine rabies clinics, state parks and inexpensive adult education programs.

51. Save on postage by using postcards, instead of letters, for short messages.

52. Keep your family healthy by paying attention to diet, exercise and cold-weather dress and limiting exposure to others who are ill.

53. Avoid incurring needless expenses on your car by performing proper maintenance. Check oil levels frequently, add antifreeze when needed and keep the gasoline tank filled so that fuel lines won't freeze in the winter.

54. Teach children to care for clothing, toys and furniture so that they don't have to be replaced as quickly as they might otherwise have to be. Keep all of your possessions in good condition and rent or share equipment that is seldom needed.

55. Reupholster or refinish furniture, particularly if you can obtain it at no or low cost from a family attic or flea market. Learn how to sew so that you'll be able to make or mend your own clothing or drapes.

56. Reduce the commission costs associated with investing by buying treasury securities directly from a Federal Reserve Bank and no-load mutual funds directly from an investment company. Use discount brokers when you don't need investment advice and prepare your own taxes, when possible (at the very least, completely organize your documentation to reduce the time a paid preparer must spend on your return). Negotiate real estate commissions, especially in a slow housing market. Get a free checking account.

57. Fix leaky faucets. A leak of one drop of water per second adds up to a loss of 2,000 gallons of water per year. A low-flow showerhead will also reduce water consumption by restricting the amount of water used during showers.

58. If you're planning to take an airline trip, investigate reduced fare options. Many airlines require that you stay over a Saturday night or fly on specific days or at specific times. If you play by their rules, the savings are substantial. Also, it is often cheaper to purchase travel packages instead of individual services (airfare, hotel, car rental, etc.) and to stay at bed-and-breakfast inns instead of hotels.

59. Swap services, such as child care, house sitting and pet feeding, with a neighbor or friend to avoid having to purchase these services privately.

60. Consider carefully answers to the questions "What do I really need?" and "What can I do without?" Is it really important to buy new clothes, have cable TV and belong to record and book clubs and a fitness center? Only you can decide what's nice and what's necessary.

Use the worksheet in Figure 6.1 to list strategies that you and your family can implement to reduce expenses. List the specific actions that can be taken and the amount of savings that can be reasonably anticipated on a *monthly* and an *annual* basis. Two examples are given.

Figure 6.1   Finding the Money To Save

Action Taken	Monthly Savings	Annual Savings
Make greater use of coupons for food shopping	$30	$360
Reduce dry cleaning	$10	$120
_____	_____	_____
_____	_____	_____
_____	_____	_____
_____	_____	_____
_____	_____	_____
_____	_____	_____
_____	_____	_____
_____	_____	_____
_____	_____	_____

Beware: At-Home and Mail-Order Shopping

Impulsive shoppers who can't trust themselves at a mall used to be able to avoid overspending by staying at home. Not anymore. Thanks to electronic-age computer wizardry, it's now possible to shop by staying home and watching television.

Shopping by television is big business and consumers are spending millions of dollars annually on items offered through television shopping networks. You simply see an object on your screen, call a toll-free number and give the operator your credit card number. Within a few weeks, the item is delivered.

Home-shopping shows often operate amidst a frenzied atmosphere. If you don't call in an order right away, you're made to feel like you're missing something. There's also not much advance notice about which items are displayed. You can't compare prices before you make a decision nor can you try on an item or see it up close. What the camera shows and what the host says are about all you have to go on.

This can add up to large credit card debts and a number of unneeded items purchased in the heat of the moment. Unless television shopping is done calmly and carefully, it may be just one more way to pile up debt.

Mail-order catalogs, too, are being used by increasing numbers of Americans. It used to be that only large department stores had a mail-order catalog. Today, thousands of specialty catalogs appeal to people who are too busy to shop in stores. Other advantages are large inventories of sizes and colors, the availability of numerous specialty items and liberal return policies.

Before ordering anything by mail, look for an address and a telephone number. Less reputable companies often have a post office box and no telephone. Read the description of the item you want to order and remember, if you're trying to match a color, that colors can be distorted in a photograph. Note the shipping times and the cost of shipping and never send cash through the mail. Most importantly, shop around. Compare prices in other catalogs and, if you have time, at local stores. You may find the item you're looking for at a lower cost closer to home.

You Can Do It

Several years ago, about 70 percent of all adults were reported to have visited a regional shopping mall at least once a week. More recently, another study found one-third of adults shopping at malls less frequently than they used to. Lack of time and money were the major reasons.

Clearly, one way to reduce spending is to stay away from malls, and home-shopping shows and mail-order catalogs. But changing behavior is never easy, as anyone who has ever broken a New Year's resolution can attest to. The key to successful behavioral changes (and New Year's resolutions) is a change in attitude. A change and its expected outcome must also be important to you personally.

Instead of spending money haphazardly, spend it by choice. At times, it will not be easy because whenever we change behavior, we cause a certain amount of discomfort in our lives. It's more comfortable not to make a change and it requires discipline to remain motivated. Reflect periodically on progress toward your financial goals to maintain, or even strengthen, your resolve.

If your resolution to spend by choice lapses, don't throw in the towel! Instead, try to determine what happened and how you can handle a similar situation in the future. You didn't walk perfectly the first time you tried. You fell. But you picked yourself up, tried again and eventually got the knack of it.

7

Your Financial Blueprint— Developing a Spending Plan That Works

It's now time to get your financial act together. You've thought about your values and goals, calculated your net worth and cash flow and read lists of ways to save more and spend less. Like a building about to be erected, you now need a blueprint, a financial blueprint, to turn your dreams into reality. That blueprint is your spending plan.

Let's begin with your financial goals. Refer to Figure 2.2 and total the amount of money needed per month to achieve short-term, intermediate-term and long-term goals. Are you presently saving enough? Probably not. Make a list of at least five ways that you could set aside more money by paying yourself first. Refer next to the cash flow worksheet in Figure 4.2. Note your expected income and expenses and any cash balance at the end of the month. If you plan any cutbacks in expenses, adjust accordingly—but be conservative, at least initially. You may not be able to cut back as much as you'd like. Then allocate your income among your expenses and make adjustments as needed.

Be sure to include savings as one of the expenses in your spending plan. If the amount of savings needed for future goals is greater than your income allows, you'll need to rework your financial goals. A larger home, an Ivy League college education for your children and a new car may not be in the cards, at least not all at once. You may have to make some choices or downsize or defer your ambitions a bit so that you can achieve all your goals but on an affordable scale.

A spending plan is an important reality test of the viability of your financial goals. It takes into account uniquely personal factors such as income and living expenses and provides a mechanism to transfer dollars from salary to savings. Remember, few people have the resources to achieve everything they'd like, all at once. Prioritize your goals and fund the most important ones first.

Remember, too, that writing some numbers on a piece of paper is no guarantee of success. A spending plan that looks good on paper often fails to work when put into action. Poor spending plans generally include one or more of the following errors:

① **No Allowance for Large Irregular Expenses—** Expenses that recur on an irregular basis include insurance premiums, tuition, vacations, holiday gifts and back-to-school clothing. Essential items such as food and health care are often cut when irregular expenses deplete available funds. It is important to plan for large variable expenses by setting aside money for them. Divide the annual expenditure by 12 and set aside the appropriate amount each month (see Figure 7.1).

② **Unrealistic Income and Expense Figures**—If you know you can't possibly manage on $150 a month for food, for example, allow more than that amount in a spending plan. The numbers used in a spending plan should closely resemble those in a recent cash flow analysis, with reasonable expense reductions, if needed. If you constantly overspend in a certain expense category, rework the numbers.

③ **Vague Expense Categories**—It's a good idea to have no more categories than you really need but avoid using such broad categories (e.g., miscellaneous expenses) that you really don't know where your money goes.

④ **No Allowance for the Unexpected**—Small emergencies, unexpected bills, office collections, school activities and charity appeals are a fact of life. A spending plan that doesn't allow a "fudge factor" for unforeseen monthly expenses is a spending plan that's doomed to fail. It is often not day-to-day expenses that strain a household's finances but unexpected bills.

⑤ **No Allowance for Inflation**—The dollar figures used in a spending plan must be updated frequently to take into account changes in household income and expenses. Auto insurance premiums can increase each time a policy is renewed and mortgage escrow accounts generally change at least once a year to reflect changes in the cost of homeowners insurance and property taxes. If the exact future cost of household expenses is unknown, err on the conservative side with a generous allowance for inflation.

Figure 7.1 Divide and Conquer Large Expenses

List the amount of irregular expenses under the month in which they occur.
Several examples are provided.

Item	Jan.	Feb.	Mar.	Apr.	May	June	July	Aug.	Sept.	Oct.	Nov.	Dec.	Add monthly figures	Divide by 12 for average monthly amount
Car insurance			$600						$600				$1,200	$100
Seasonal clothing				$500					$500				$1,000	$85
Vacation								$500				$100	$600	$50
Totals														

Spending Plans That Work

A spending plan is nothing more than a personalized system for matching income and expenses. It requires no special forms (any blank sheet of paper will do) and no special training. A hand-held calculator is nice but not necessary and a computer is helpful but still requires human input and planning.

No one right way to set up a spending plan exists and what works for one person may not work for another. The most important thing is to base future spending on what you actually spent in the past. Three basic types of spending plans often used, with individual variations, include the account method, the running balance method and the spreadsheet method.

The Account Method

The account method, also known as the declining balance method, is an updated version of a money management system that was popular early this century. People often divided their cash among a collection of envelopes, with an envelope earmarked for each expense category. When the money in an envelope was gone, spending in that category ceased unless funds were transferred from another envelope. Eventually, it became very cumbersome to make notations of transfers between accounts on the envelopes and, besides, envelopes pay no interest.

The account method spending plan is analogous to having a series of envelopes for household expenses. Each paycheck is apportioned on paper among various expenses (e.g., rent—$500; utilities—$200). The actual cash is placed in a checking or savings account, however, instead of envelopes. When money is spent in a particular category, the amount is subtracted from the account balance, just as if cash were physically removed from an envelope. This way, it is always clear how much money remains in each expense category.

Surpluses or deficits in each account, including an account for unforeseen expenses, are carried foward from each month to the next. For instance, if $30 had been allotted for the telephone bill and only $20 spent, the next month would have a total of $40 in this category ($10 remaining plus the next month's $30). The account method usually works well unless borrowing between accounts is excessive and the total amount spent exceeds the total amount allotted to all expense categories. Figure 7.2 shows what a typical month's account method spending plan would look like with just a few sample entries of household expenses.

The Running Balance Method

The running balance method is similar to the account method in that balances carry forward from one month to the next. Instead of keeping track of individual expense categories, however, this method tracks only the total surplus or deficit in household spending. To develop a running balance spending plan, you need three things: a

Figure 7.2 April Account Method Spending Plan

Previous Balance	Sav- ings $5,000	Hous- ing $320	Food $250	Loans $50	Util- lities −$30	Misc. $200
April 1			−100		−80	
Bills			150		−110	
April 8			−100			
Bills			50			
April 13	+100	+300	+250	+100	+150	+50
Paycheck	5,100	620	300	150	40	250
April 15			−100		−30	−200
Bills			200		10	50
April 22		−20	−100	−180		
Bills		600	100	−30		
April 27	+100	+300	+250	+100	+150	+50
Paycheck	5,200	900	350	70	160	100
April 29		-575	−100	−30	−140	
Bills		325	250	40	20	
Balance	$5,200	$325	$250	$40	$20	$100

recent cash flow statement, a list of due dates for irregular expenses and a calendar to indicate the days of the month that family members get paid. Projections can then be made at one sitting for a three-month to twelve-month period.

The running balance method conveniently allows for the build-up of funds to pay large irregular expenses

Figure 7.3 January Running Balance Spending Plan

Balance at end of previous month	$265	
January 1 bills	($250)—$	15
Husband's January 3 paycheck	$200 —$	215
Wife's January 3 paycheck	$400 —$	615
Husband's January 10 paycheck	$200 —$	815
January 10 bills	($100)—$	715
Husband's January 17 paycheck	$200 —$	915
Wife's January 17 paycheck	$400 —$	,315
January 17 bills	($100)—$	1,215
Auto insurance premium	($400)—$	815
Husband's January 24 paycheck	$200 —$	1,015
January 24 bills	($100)—$	915
Husband's January 31 paycheck	$200 —$	1,115
Wife's January 31 paycheck	$400 —$	1,515
January 31 bills	($850)—$	665
Reserve for unforeseen expenses	($100)—$	565
Balance carried over to following month	$565	

and for savings from those extra paychecks discussed in Chapter 5. Figure 7.3 provides a sample running balance spending plan for one month for a two-paycheck couple.

Naturally, with this method the minimum amount of money set aside each month must equal routine monthly expenses plus one-twelfth of large annual expenses. Note that the husband was paid weekly and the wife, biweekly. Each received an extra paycheck during this particular month. Funds from such checks can be either placed directly into savings or included, as shown in Figure 7.3, as part of monthly household income. This helps build a surplus for large variable expenses such as auto insurance. The couple also included a $100-a-month reserve in their spending plan for unforeseen expenses. If it is needed, the money will be spent. If it is not, funds should be transferred to an interest-bearing account as a reserve for future emergencies.

Every three to twelve months, a continuation of the current running balance spending plan should be developed using up-to-date income and expense figures and carrying forward the ending balance of the previous plan. If the balance carried forward gradually comes to exceed, say, $500, part of the excess should be placed in savings.

The Spreadsheet Method

The spreadsheet method spending plan is nothing more than an extension of a recent cash flow statement. Using the categories identified in Figure 4.2, make two columns on a piece of paper with the headings "target amount" and "actual amount." Fill in the target amount column at the beginning of the month with the amount of your anticipated income and the amount allotted to each expense category. At the end of the month, enter what you actually earned and spent (you can get the information from your paycheck stubs and checkbook) in the actual amount column and compare the two figures.

With the spreadsheet method, it is also important to anticipate the months with extra paychecks and irregular expenses. You can use a sheet of paper for each month's calculation or, better still, buy a pad of bookkeepers ledger paper and enter an entire year's worth of calculations on one page. This helps you see at a glance seasonal variations in spending and the surplus or deficit carried over from one month to the next. Spreadsheets can also be done on a computer with an accounting program such as LOTUS 1-2-3 or one of several available personal finance software packages. Computer programs often calculate year-to-date income and expense totals automatically and run projections of what each spending plan category will look like at the end of the year.

Figure 7.4 provides a spreadsheet method spending plan for a two-month period with some sample income and expense categories.

10 Tips for a Better Spending Plan

① **Include Savings**—You must think of savings as an expense and not as something to do with money that is left over. Savings can be taken off the top and automatically deposited in a credit union or an employer savings plan, or it can be included as a household expense in a spending plan and paid immediately (to yourself). Persons who methodically save 5 to 10 percent (or more) of their income instead of saving whatever is left over at

Figure 7.4 November/December Spreadsheet Method Spending Plan

	November Target Amount	November Actual Amount	December Target Amount	December Actual Amount
Income				
Husband's net				
Salary	$900	$1,000*	$900	$900
Wife's net				
Salary	900	900	1,400	1,200*
Interest	35	40	40	40
Other	—	150**	—	—
	$1,835	$2,090	$2,340	$2,140

*Includes overtime *Includes holiday bonus
**50/50 raffle prize

Expenses				
Savings	$250	$250	$250	$250
Mortgage	655	655	655	655
Utilities	205	245	235	275
Loans and Credit	145	165	245	250
Insurance	170	170	0	0
Food	300	280	300	320
Transportation	80	100	80	85
Other	50	85	150	250
Total	$1,855	$1,950	$1,915	$2,085
Surplus or deficit	<20>	140	425	55

the end of the month will progress steadily toward achieving their financial goals.

② **Include Some Discretionary Income**—Each family member should have a certain amount of money included in the spending plan that is his or hers to spend as that person pleases (this is where the element of spending by choice comes in). The freedom to make small purchases without consulting anyone will keep a spending plan from feeling like a financial straight jacket and help avoid conflicts when spending values differ.

③ **Check Your Math**—Make sure that the total amount allotted for all expense categories, including savings, does not exceed your household's total monthly after-tax income. Unless expenses are kept in check, a spending plan will fail.

④ **Review and Revise**—Don't be discouraged if some of your income and expense estimates are off in the beginning and be prepared to make adjustments from month to month. Comparing estimated and actual spending amounts provides valuable feedback about areas of a spending plan that need improvement.

⑤ **Juggle, Juggle, Juggle**—Whenever you spend extra money in one category, try to cut an equal amount somewhere else. Including a reserve in each month's spending plan will also help keep the bottom line in the black.

⑥ **Keep It Simple**—Spending plans are best handled on a month-to-month basis, even though some expenses are paid weekly, quarterly, semiannually or annually. With a monthly plan, it is easier to see exactly where you stand and to make revisions as they are needed.

⑦ **Be Positive**—A person's pyschological reaction to a spending plan is important. The more positive the approach, the better. A spending plan should be viewed as a document that spells out what you can do, not one that says you can't.

⑧ **Try, Try Again**—It often takes some time and effort to keep each expense category comfortable, include savings for future goals and not exceed available take-home pay. Be prepared to try different scenarios until you find one that works.

⑨ **Avoid Quick Fixes**—It may be tempting to eliminate an entire category of spending in order to make income and expense figures jive. Don't do it! The figures will look good on paper but you'll wind up frustrated and resentful about having to give up an expense that was formerly very important. Instead, try to trim several expenses by smaller amounts. That way, some money will still be available for all of the things you enjoy.

⑩ **Allow Time**—Remember, you'll be breaking habits that have been in existence for years. You cannot expect a transformation overnight but you should see steady progress.

The Fudge-It Budget

Yes, I promised not to use the word *budget* but the rhyme was just too tempting! Hopefully, by now you realize that the difference between the words *budget* and *spending plan* is more than semantics. Spending plans work because the individuals who prepare them control their financial destiny. They make decisions based on both personal choices and available income. Money for fun and a reserve for unanticipated expenses are included as part of the plan.

No one can tell you what your lifestyle ought to be or how you should spend your money. If it's important to your family to go out to dinner together at least once a week, you will probably spend more on food than other families do. But if dining out brings great pleasure, it might be a mistake to make major cutbacks in this expense category. Instead, spend less money on something else to keep your spending plan on track. Another family, on the other hand, might consider a two-week vacation in the mountains more important and eating out a luxury it can do without.

Because life is full of unexpected events, every spending plan needs a fudge factor. This is an amount of money that can be used for anything that is unexpected and deemed important. Between $50 and $200 a month should be sufficient for most households. People with a fudge factor in their spending plan won't have to raid their savings account or use a credit card to pay these unanticipated bills.

Once you've allocated funds for a particular item, you may need to do without something else. Think about that in relation to where you are now and where you want to be five or ten years from now. Then develop a spending plan that reflects the values and goals that you and your family feel are important. If you know how much money you have and how much you need, you are in an excellent position to take charge of your finances.

8

Earlybirds Get the Worm— Maximizing the Time Value of Money

The value of a dollar today is different than its value tomorrow. Today's dollar will be worth more in the future because it can be saved or invested to earn interest. Future value is the amount that a sum of money will be worth at a later date when it is compounded for a given time period at a given interest rate. The longer the compounding period and the higher the interest rate, the larger the future value.

When you are saving money to achieve financial goals, time is a very important ally. The earlier you start saving, the more you can take advantage of the effects of compounding, or the time value of money. For example, if you can earn a net interest rate of 2 percent after inflation, for every dollar you need in 20 years, you would need to save only 67 cents now. If you need that same dollar in 10 years instead of 20, you'd need to set aside 82 cents. And if you need that dollar in five years, you'd have to set aside 91 cents. When you're ten years or less away from a long-term goal, the savings required are substantial because your money has less time to grow.

The time value of money is especially impressive in a tax-deferred investment such as an annuity or individual retirement account (IRA). To illustrate this point, let's compare two IRA owners. One contributes $2,000 a year for six years between the ages of 22 and 28. The other makes an initial contribution at age 29 and contributes $2,000 a year through age 65. Assuming an average annual return of 12 percent in growth-oriented investments, the IRA funded with six years of early contributions and the IRA funded later over 36 years would be worth about the same.

It's important to remember that compound interest is *not* retroactive. It is difficult to make up in your 60s for the savings you could have accumulated decades earlier. To enjoy the benefits of the time value of money, start saving today. Saving $3,000 a year at 8 percent for 10, 20 and 30 years will total $43,460, $137,285 and $339,850, respectively. Waiting a decade to start saving can mean a difference of more than $200,000!

The decisions that people make to spend and save money affect the way their money accumulates. Let's take the purchase of a car. The difference between a $15,000 car and a $20,000 car is a lot more than $5,000. Assuming an interest rate of 10 percent, borrowing $15,000 over five years will cost $319 a month while borrowing $20,000 will cost $425. If the difference, $106 a month, were saved for ten years and earned an 8 percent average rate of return, the owner of the less expensive car (another option would be a late-model "gently used" car) would have an additional $20,000.

Planning Ahead with Time on Your Side

The time value of money can work both *for* you and *against* you. On the positive side, it will increase the value of a given amount of savings. Conversely, the cost of goods and services will also increase through inflation. The earlier you start saving for a financial goal, the less costly and burdensome it will be. You'll also need to save less money per month if you can earn a higher yield on savings and investments. Financial planners often use time value charts to calculate how much a goal will cost in the future, assuming a given rate of inflation, and how much money must be saved per month and per year at a given rate of interest.

Any time value calculation is only as good as the assumptions that underlie it. Therefore, it is best to err on the conservative side when making predictions. Thus, let's assume a 6 percent average annual inflation rate in Figure 8.1. To find the factor by which inflation will increase the cost of goods and services over the years, select the appropriate deadline in the "Years to Goal" column and find the corresponding future value factor in the "Inflation Factor" column.

Multiplying the current cost of a financial goal by the appropriate inflation factor gives you its estimated future cost (you could also use the rule of 72 but time value charts are more precise). If your goal is to buy a new car

Figure 8.1 Future Value Factors

Years to Goal	6% Inflation Factor	Years to Goal	6% Inflation Factor
1	1.06	16	2.54
2	1.12	17	2.69
3	1.19	18	2.85
4	1.26	19	3.03
5	1.34	20	3.21
6	1.42	21	3.40
7	1.50	22	3.60
8	1.59	23	3.82
9	1.69	24	4.05
10	1.79	25	4.30
11	1.89	26	4.55
12	2.01	27	4.82
13	2.13	28	5.11
14	2.26	29	5.42
15	2.40	30	5.74

that costs $14,000 today in five years, its cost then will be $18,760 ($14,000 times 1.34).

Once you've determined the future cost of a financial goal, you can use a future value of annuity table to determine how much you must save on an annual and a monthly basis. You must assume some rate of return to estimate the required savings. To determine the factor by

Figure 8.2 6 Percent Future Value of Annuity Factors

Years to Goal	6% Rate of Return	Years to Goal	6% Rate of Return
1	1.00	16	25.67
2	2.06	17	28.21
3	3.18	18	30.91
4	4.37	19	33.76
5	5.64	20	36.79
6	6.98	21	39.99
7	8.39	22	43.39
8	9.90	23	46.99
9	11.49	24	50.82
10	13.18	25	54.86
11	14.97	26	59.16
12	16.87	27	63.71
13	18.88	28	68.53
14	21.02	29	73.64
15	23.28	30	79.06

which a given rate of return, compounded annually, increases the value of an investment, select the appropriate figure from the left-hand column and find the return rate factor to the right. Figures 8.2, 8.3 and 8.4 provide three tables that assume a 6, 8 and 10 percent return, respectively, on savings and investments.

So what will a future goal cost and how much savings

Figure 8.3   8 Percent Future Value of Annuity Factors

Years to Goal	6% Inflation Factor	Years to Goal	6% Inflation Factor
1	1.00	16	30.32
2	2.08	17	33.75
3	3.25	18	37.45
4	4.50	19	41.45
5	5.87	20	45.76
6	7.33	21	50.42
7	8.92	22	55.46
8	10.64	23	60.89
9	12.49	24	66.76
10	14.49	25	73.10
11	16.64	26	79.95
12	18.98	27	87.35
13	21.50	28	95.34
14	24.21	29	103.96
15	27.15	30	113.28

is needed? Figure 8.5 shows you, using each of the time value factor tables in Figures 8.1 through 8.4. An example of the Jones family, who is saving to buy a car, is given as an illustration.

As the example in Figure 8.5 indicates, you'll need to save more money each month to reach a given goal if the yield on savings is reduced. Another factor to consider is

Figure 8.4   10 Percent Future Value of Annuity Factors

Years to Goal	6% Inflation Factor	Years to Goal	6% Inflation Factor
1	1.00	16	35.95
2	2.10	17	40.54
3	3.31	18	45.60
4	4.64	19	51.16
5	6.10	20	57.27
6	7.71	21	64.00
7	9.49	22	71.40
8	11.43	23	79.54
9	13.58	24	88.50
10	15.94	25	98.35
11	18.53	26	109.18
12	21.38	27	121.10
13	24.52	28	134.21
14	27.97	29	148.63
15	31.77	30	164.49

the compounding period. The effect of compounding is that interest is earned on interest. The more often interest is compounded, the faster a given sum of money will grow. In other words, all other things equal, daily compounding pays more than monthly compounding, monthly more than quarterly, quarterly more than semiannually and semiannually more than annually.

Figure 8.5   Time Value of Money Worksheet

	You	The Joneses
1. Number of years to financial goal	_____	5
2. Cost of financial goal today	_____	$14,000
3. Inflation factor. Refer to Figure 8.1 for the inflation factor based on the time horizon indicated in Step 1.	_____	1.34
4. Future annual cost of goal. Multiply Step 2 by Step 3	_____	$18,760
5. Amount of savings needed, assuming a *6 percent* average yield:		
a) Using the number of years left until the goal, refer to Figure 8.2 and enter the applicable return rate factor	_____	5.64
b) Annual amount to save. Divide Step 5a into Step 4	_____	$3,326
c) Monthly amount to save. Divide Step 5b by 12.	_____	$277

Figure 8.5   Time Value of Money Worksheet (Continued)

	You	The Joneses
6. Amount of savings needed, assuming an *8 percent* average yield:		
a) Using the number of years left until the goal, refer to Figure 8.3 and enter the applicable return rate factor.	_____	5.87
b) Annual amount to save. Divide Step 6a into Step 4	_____	$3,196
c) Monthly amount to save. Divide Step 6b by 12.	_____	$266
7. Amount of savings needed, assuming a *10 percent* average yield:		
a) Using the number of years left until the goal, refer to Figure 8.4 and enter the applicable return rate factor.	_____	6.10
b) Annual amount to save. Divide Step 7a into Step 4	_____	$3,075
c) Monthly amount to save. Divide Step 7b by 12.	_____	$256

How To Beat Inflation and Taxes

Do you know what a house, a car or even a loaf of bread will cost 10 or 20 years from now? The answer is: a lot more than they do today. It is a sad fact of life that expenses don't stay constant. Thanks to inflation, a dollar today will not be worth as much in the future. If the thought of having to save large amounts of money sounds depressing, don't despair! Remember, incomes more or less keep pace with prices. Do you remember when gasoline cost less than 50 cents a gallon? The fact that people are still able to afford to drive shows our ability to adjust to price changes. The key is to try to earn an average after-tax yield on savings and investments that matches or exceeds the rate of inflation. If the after-tax return on savings and investments is greater than or equal to the inflation rate over the long run, you'll retain purchasing power. In Chapter 1, the formula used to determine the return needed to break even after taxes and inflation was explained.

Many people choose to move their money from savings products to investments to receive a higher return and to achieve steady growth over time. This is a major difference between savings and investments. With *savings*, your principal remains intact and earns a designated rate of return. With *investments*, your capital may or may not increase in value and the rate of return is unknown.

Examples of investment products include real estate, stocks, mutual funds, variable annuities, bonds and collectibles such as coins, stamps and antiques. As a general rule, the higher the rate of return, the greater the risk. But the difference between a 3 percent and an 8 percent return, compounded over time, can make a big difference in your financial security.

Making the Leap from Saver to Investor

Did you ever wish that there was a perfect investment? One that paid a high yield (15 percent or more would be nice), entailed little risk and was free from federal and state taxes? Unfortunately, no such thing as a perfect investment exists. Lower risk products, such as certificates of deposit (CDs), fixed annuities and money market mutual funds, yield only mediocre returns and stocks and growth mutual funds that have the potential to appreciate are fully taxable. Tax reform has also changed the advantages of certain investments relative to others. Long-term capital gains from the sale of stock and mutual funds have been fully taxable since 1987.

Two things to consider carefully before investing your money *anywhere* are your *risk tolerance level* and your *knowledge* about a specific investment product. If you don't understand an investment or you feel uncomfortable and worried, it is not a good place for your money. The deadline for your financial goals also must be considered. If your goals are ten years or more in the future, you have time for an investment to fully appreciate or to recoup any potential losses.

Another consideration is your marginal tax bracket.

Persons in higher tax brackets often earn a greater
return with tax-exempt investment products such as
municipal bonds, bond mutual funds and bond unit
trusts than with taxable products. Figure 8.6 indicates
the taxable equivalent rates for tax-exempt investments
for households in the 15, 28 and 31 percent marginal
tax brackets.

Another wise strategy is to diversify your investments
among several types of products to reduce the risk of
making a poor selection. Financial professionals refer to
the process of putting money in different asset classes

Figure 8.6 Tax-Exempt and Taxable Yields

	Taxable Equivalent Yield		
Tax-Exempt Yield	15% Bracket	28% Bracket	31% Bracket
2.0%	2.35%	2.77%	2.90%
2.5	2.94	3.47	3.62
3.0	3.53	4.17	4.35
3.5	4.18	4.86	5.07
4.0	4.71	5.55	5.80
4.5	5.29	6.25	6.52
5.0	5.88	6.94	7.25
5.5	6.47	7.64	7.97
6.0	7.06	8.33	8.70
6.5	7.65	9.03	9.42
7.0	8.24	9.72	10.14
7.5	8.82	10.42	10.87
8.0	9.41	11.11	11.59

with different characteristics as asset allocation. As an example, a portfolio might be 50 percent invested in equities yielding 10 percent, 30 percent invested in bonds yielding 8 percent and 20 percent invested in cash equivalents earning 3.5 percent. The average return on the portfolio would be 8.1 percent ($[50 \times .10] + [30 \times .08] + [20 \times .035] = 8.1$). A well-balanced portfolio will, over time, produce greater yields than very conservative investment products alone but will have less risk and volatility than a portfolio of more speculative investments.

Persons planning to invest money for future financial goals should consider the following:

① **Seek Assistance**—Periodicals such as *MONEY, Worth, Barron's* and *The Wall Street Journal* are available at most public libraries. Another source of information are television programs like "Wall Street Week." Financial professionals, such as a stockbroker, can also provide helpful information.

② **Be Consistent**—Dollar cost average by depositing in an investment a fixed amount of money on a regular basis (e.g., $100 a month in a mutual fund).

③ **Be Realistic**—Few people ever make a killing on their investments. Deals that sound too good to be true usually are.

④ **Review and Revise**—As financial goals are achieved and new ones develop, be prepared to revise your investment portfolio. Changes in the economy and tax laws may also require periodic changes in plans.

⑤ **Keep Records**—Good records are important for both tax purposes and to analyze the performance of investments.

Financial planners often use the investment pyramid concept to describe the risk and reward potential of various investments (see Figure 8.7). In general, the higher the rate of return sought (using investments in the top two-thirds of the pyramid), the more risk investors must be willing to assume. The bottom third of the pyramid depicts products where safety of principal is guaranteed or the risk of loss is reduced.

Evaluate Your Risk Tolerance Level

Among the factors that affect an investor's risk tolerance level are age, income, amount of assets and liabilities, investment knowledge and experience, and the deadline for achievement of financial goals. Generally speaking, younger investors and those with substantial assets and incomes can afford to take more risk (investing $5,000 of an $80,000 portfolio is a lot different than investing your only $5,000). Also, as investors expand their knowledge of the risks and rewards of specific products, their risk tolerance level rises.

See Figure 8.8 for a quiz to help you determine how much risk you are comfortable with. The higher the score, the more resources (time, money, knowledge, etc.) you have to increase your capacity to handle investment risk.

Figure 8.7 The Investment Pyramid

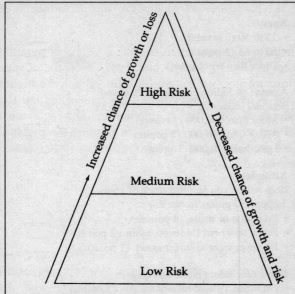

Increased chance of growth or loss

Decreased chance of growth and risk

High Risk

Medium Risk

Low Risk

- Futures/ options
- Speculative stocks
- Lower grade bonds
- Collectibles

- Blue chip stocks
- High-grade corporate/ municipal bonds
- Real estate
- Mutual funds
- Annuities (variable)

- Passbooks
- CDs
- Money market accounts/funds
- Life insurance cash value
- Annuities (fixed)
- Treasury securities
- Home equity
- Insured checking/ savings accounts
- EE and HH bonds
- Pension plan funds

Figure 8.8   Determining Your Risk Tolerance

1. **Age:**
   - 25 to 50 (3 points)   _____
   - 50 to 65 (2 points)   _____
   - Older than 65 (1 point)

2. **Assets** (excluding emergency fund and personal property):
   - More than $50,000 (3 points)   _____
   - $20,000 to $50,000 (2 points)   _____
   - Less than $20,000 (1 point)

3. **Attitude:**
   How would you feel if a stock of yours dropped 50 points in one day?
   - I'd take it in stride. (3 points)   _____
   - I'd be upset but I'd invest again. (2 points)   _____
   - I'd never want to invest again. (1 point)

4. **Debts** (excluding home mortgage):
   - Less than 10% of take-home pay (3 points)   _____
   - 10% to 15% of take-home pay (2 points)   _____
   - More than 15% of take-home pay (1 point)

5. **Emergency fund:**
   - More than six months' expenses (3 points)   _____
   - Three to six months' expenses (2 points)   _____
   - Less than three months' expenses (1 point)

6. **Feelings about the Future of the U.S. Economy:**
   - Optimistic (3 points)   _____
   - Unsure (2 points)   _____
   - Pessimistic (1 point)   _____

Figure 8.8   Determining Your Risk Tolerance (Continued)

---

7. **Annual household Income:**
   - More than $60,000 (3 points)   ___
   - Between $30,000 and $60,000 (2 points)   ___
   - Less than $30,000 (1 point)   ___

8. **Knowledge and experience level:**
   - Knowledge, calm and self-assured
     (3 points)   ___
   - Some investment knowledge and
     experience (2 points)   ___
   - Little knowledge or experience (1 point)

9. **Present investment portfolio:**   ___
   - Mostly real estate, stock, growth funds
     (3 points)   ___
   - Mostly bonds, annuities, treasuries
     (2 points)   ___
   - Mostly CDs, money market accounts
     (1 point)   ___

10. **Deadline for financial goal:**   ___
    - Ten years or more away (3 points)   ___
    - Three to ten years away (2 points)
    - Less than three years away (1 point)

If your score totals 23 points or more, you are in a
good position to increase your tolerance for risk. A score
of 15 to 23 points indicates a moderate risk tolerance
level and a total of fewer than 15 points, a low risk tolerance level.

Time diversification is a term used by financial planners to describe the reduction of investment risk that
often accompanies the lengthening of an investment's

holding period. A number of research studies have concluded that the risk associated with a particular investment decreases as the holding period increases. As an example, stocks have had returns ranging from ‾43 percent to 54 percent during one-year time periods between 1926 and 1991. Over this entire period, however, the stocks' return was 10.4 percent, more than twice that of bonds or cash equivalents.

What this means is that financial goals must be clearly defined *before* any savings or investment product is selected. The deadline of a goal must match the holding period of an investment. Never fund a long-term goal (e.g., retirement) with a short-term product (e.g., money market fund) or a short-term goal (e.g., closing costs for a house) with a long-term product (e.g., stock). Assets in the upper two-thirds of the investment pyramid may be less risky than they would otherwise be, however, if they are held long term in a diversified portfolio.

Clearly, time can be one of a saver's best friends. Not only can it reduce the long-term risk of certain investments but, combined with a systematic savings habit and products that earn more than the rate of inflation, it can produce spectacular growth, especially if money is given two or more decades to compound. Yes, time plus money equals magic, and people of average means can become wealthy with time on their side. For example, if you earn $35,000 annually and save 10 percent ($3,500), earning 9 percent, for 35 years, you'll have more than $750,000. If the amount of savings is steadily increased in step with cost-of-living wage adjustments or promotions, you could retire a millionaire!

9

In Debt or Over Your Head? How To Avoid a Credit Crunch

Credit, very simply, is the present use of future income. A fee or finance charge is assessed for the privilege of borrowing money for a specified time. Available borrowing vehicles include home mortgages, car loans, home equity lines of credit and credit cards. Between 1980 and 1990, household debt increased at a rate of 10 percent per year. At the end of 1990, Americans owed about $800 billion, excluding home mortgages. It has been estimated that 70 percent of U.S. families today have at least one credit card, up from 50 percent in 1970. It's also not unusual for credit card users to have both a Mastercard and a Visa or perhaps two or more of each. A decade ago, about half of all cardholders paid their balances in full each month. Today, fewer than 30 percent do. The average balance carried in mid-1993 was about $1,650.

Increased debt is a major reason for the low rate of savings in this country. Many consumers carry debt in excess of 20 percent of take-home pay, which is considered an extremely high level. Economists are divided as to whether consumers are in over their heads. It depends to a large degree on the stability of income and assets of the people doing the borrowing. Illness or unemployment could put many families living on the edge in serious jeopardy. Even for those who have a secure job and an adequate emergency fund, the cost of credit is high. The average rate charged on bank credit cards in late 1993 was 17.01 percent, more than five times the yield of a typical passbook savings account. With every $100 of debt costing $17 in interest, revolving a balance can add significantly to the cost of goods and services purchased on credit.

Nevertheless, credit has its advantages. It allows people to immediately purchase products on sale, pay for several items together with one check, use goods and services while they are being paid for and avoid having to spend money on items for which employer reimbursement is expected. Borrowing money also helps establish a credit rating (credit often gives you access to more credit) and is helpful in emergencies, with telephone orders or mail-order shopping and as leverage for disputes with merchants. Many people also charge purchases because they find it easier to repay a loan than replenish a savings account. Others expecting a gift, a bonus or their next pay-check charge purchases, which they plan to pay off in full, in anticipation of the future income.

A major disadvantage of credit, in addition to its cost, is its encouragement of impulse buying and overspending by some people. This can lead to serious problems, such as repossession of purchased items, garnishment of wages and bankruptcy. Credit also ties up future income with debt sometimes long outlasting the items that it purchased. For this reason, credit cards should not be used to charge meals, except in business-related situations (many people are paying 18 to 21 percent interest on meals they can't remember eating). If home equity lines of credit are used to purchase a car, they should be paid off over the useful life of the vehicle. A final disadvantage of credit is that its true cost has increased with the phase-out of consumer interest as an itemized tax deduction.

Two basic types of credit exist: open-ended and closed-ended. Both can cause serious financial problems if used carelessly. Open-ended loans, also known as revolving credit, give a borrower the right to make purchases on a continuous basis, up to a specified maximum limit. Bills are issued monthly for the amount currently owed, plus interest. Examples of open-ended loans are home equity lines of credit, credit cards and checking account overdraft plans.

Closed-end loans, on the other hand, establish in advance just how much money is owed each month. They are used most often to make one-time purchases of expensive items like furniture, major appliances and cars. The payment period, number of payments and cost per month remain fixed for the life of the loan. Car loans, second mortgages and home improvement loans are closed-ended.

Read the Fine Print

Do you know what credit costs? You should! There's no such thing as a free lunch and finance charges and loan terms vary from lender to lender. It's important to shop around for the best buys on credit, just as you would for a car, a blouse or a plumber. A 7 percent, $5,000, five-year loan, secured by a bank account or certificate of deposit (CD), costs $99 a month compared to $114 a month for a similar but unsecured loan charging 13 percent. At the end of the loan period, the borrower paying 7 percent would have saved $900.

Several federal laws provide important benefits to consumers. One of the most important is the Truth-in-Lending section of the 1968 Consumer Credit Protection Act. The Truth-in-Lending Law requires creditors to tell applicants in simple language what a loan will cost so that comparisons among lenders can be made. The Fair Credit Reporting Act (1970) requires that consumers be given the name and address of the credit bureau whose report was used as a basis for the denial of credit. The Equal Credit Opportunity Act (1974) prohibits creditors from discriminating against applicants and existing customers on the basis of factors such as age, race, gender or marital status. The Fair Credit and Charge Card Disclosure Act (1988) requires credit card issuers to disclose credit terms on applications and solicitation materials rather than after applications are approved.

One of the most important credit decisions consumers can make is their choice of a credit card. The average American adult has eight credit cards, 2.5 of which are bank cards. With the market for new cardholders reaching a saturation point, credit card companies offer enticements such as cash rebates, frequent flyer miles and merchandise discounts to lure away each others' customers. Chances are you have received offers in the mail asking whether you would like to apply for a new credit card (federal law prohibits creditors from sending an actual credit card unless you request it). Frequently, these offers say that you've been preapproved for a specific line of credit but only if you apply quickly, before the offer expires. Creditors usually get your name by paying a credit reporting agency for the names and addresses of people who fit a predetermined profile.

A recent study found that six in ten credit card users had no idea how much interest they paid the previous year on their credit card bills. Paying more than is necessary could cost thousands of dollars over a lifetime. Before accepting any credit card offer, study the terms and conditions that apply. These terms, along with the interest rate, determine the cost you'll pay for borrowing money. Below are six factors to consider:

① **Annual Percentage Rate**—The annual percentage rate (APR) is the total cost of credit expressed on an annual basis. According to federal law, the APR must be disclosed on charge card applications and monthly billing statements. The APR is helpful when comparison shopping for the least expensive credit card or installment loan. A credit card charging a seemingly innocuous 1.65 percent a month carries an APR of 19.8 percent.

② **Annual Fees**—Many bank card issuers charge an annual fee of $20 to $35 for standard credit cards and from $50 to $100 for premium, or gold, credit cards. Since 1989, credit card issuers have been required to dis-

close information about annual fees and other charges at
the time of credit card solicitation and application.

③ **Transaction Fees**—Some credit card issuers also
charge a fee when you use their card to obtain a cash
advance, exceed your credit limit or send in a late payment. Others charge a flat monthly fee of $2 to $5
whether you use the credit card or not.

④ **A Grace Period**—A grace period allows borrowers to avoid a finance charge by paying their current balance in full before the due date. If a credit card has a
grace period, the issuer must mail a bill at least 14 days
before the payment is due to ensure that there's enough
time to make a payment. Some credit card issuers have
lowered their interest rate from 21 to as low as 9 to 14
percent and eliminated or reduced their annual fee. What
they have done instead, however, is eliminate their grace
period. Some credit cards without grace periods charge
interest from the date of purchase while others charge
interest from the date a purchase is posted to an account.
The idea, of course, is to collect interest from all cardholders, not just those who revolve a balance. Even if
you pay in full upon receipt of a statement, you'll still
owe some interest.

⑤ **Balance Computation Method**—It is important
to understand how a credit card issuer calculates finance
charges. Like the APR, the finance charge computation
method must be disclosed to consumers. The method
used can make a big difference in the amount owed,
even when the APR is identical to that of another credit
card. The most advantageous method for consumers is

the adjusted balance method. The balance, on which interest is assessed, is computed by subtracting payments made during a billing period from the balance owed at the end of the previous billing period. New purchases are not included. The most common method used by credit card issuers is the **average daily balance method**. This method, too, gives borrowers credit for recent payments and may or may not include new purchases. To compute the finance charge, a card issuer totals the balance for each day in the billing period, adds the balances together and divides the total by the number of days. The resulting figure is the average daily balance on which a finance charge is levied. One of the least advantageous methods for consumers is the **previous balance method**. This is where creditors assess finance charges on the previous balance before subtracting any payments.

In recent years, changing balance computation practices have exacerbated Americans' debt problems. Two examples are (1) the reduction in required minimum payments from 4 to 5 percent of the outstanding balance to 2 to 3 percent and (2) the use of two-cycle average daily balance calculations that add the average daily balances for two billing cycles: the current cycle and the previous one. The two-cycle method is generally the most expensive way to calculate the balance on which interest is charged, especially when new purchases are added to the current billing cycle.

⑥ **Bells and Whistles**—Airline credit cards and cards issued by nonbanks such as General Motors and Ford provide substantial bonuses, particularly for those who charge heavily. Airlines credit one frequent flyer mile for every dollar spent while other issuers provide rebates for future purchases. Givebacks often exceed the cost of these enhanced credit cards for people who charge frequently and pay their bills in full. For those who carry a balance, however, they can be an expensive proposition. Bankcard Holders of America recently compared a 15.9 percent airline credit card to one offered by a bank charging 8.9 percent and assumed that a consumer charged $20,000 in a year and earned a free trip. In this case, the consumer was clearly a winner. If the consumer paid only half the bill, however, and carried a $10,000 balance, he or she would pay $1,590 in annual interest and a $60 dollar annual fee versus $890 in interest and a $39 annual fee for the low-rate card. The consumer's free trip just cost $721!

The type of credit card you use should match your debt repayment habits. If you're one of the 28 percent of users who pay their bill in full each month, look for a credit card with a low or no annual fee and at least a 25-day grace period. If you regularly carry over a balance from month to month, choose a credit card with a low interest rate and an adjusted or a one-cycle average daily balance computation method. If you alternate between full and partial payments, seek out a low interest rate and a grace period.

10 Credit Management Tips

Like many things in life, credit can be a help or a hindrance, depending on how it is used. The key to effective debt management is selecting loans with the lowest rates and most favorable terms and paying bills promptly to keep finance charges as low as possible. Below are ten additional tips to consider:

① **Don't Go Overboard**—Use Figure 9.1 to list your present debt obligations. If your total monthly payments are larger than one-fifth (20 percent) of your monthly take-home pay, your debt load is at a dangerous level. You'll need to stop incurring new debts and eliminate outstanding debts as quickly as possible. For a safe level of outstanding credit, households should commit no more than 10 percent of monthly take-home pay (excluding a mortgage) to debt repayment. A household bringing home $2,500 a month ($30,000 annually), for example, should aim to owe no more than $250 a month. Don't allow credit card bills to exceed what you can afford to repay. Set a maximum dollar limit and stick to it.

② **Set Your Own Terms**—Borrow *only* the amount of money you need and shorten the length of the loan, when possible. If a financial institution won't make a loan for less than $1,000 and you need only for example, $800, repay the additional $200 immediately to decrease the finance charge. If you use a 15-year or 20-year home equity loan to purchase a car, use a three-year to five-year loan repayment schedule so that the loan is repaid while the car still runs. It is often possible to make adjustments in loan repayments and still comply with a lender's overall regulations.

Figure 9.1 Evaluate Your Credit Status

Use this worksheet to total your present debt obligations (excluding a mortgage). Fill in all the blanks that apply, using information from loan contracts or credit card billing statements. Then compare your debt load to the suggested percentages listed below.

Type of Loan	Amount Still Owed	APR %	Months Left To Pay	Amt. of Monthly Payment
Bank card(s)	_____	_____	_____	_____
Car loan(s)	_____	_____	_____	_____
Checking account overdraft	_____	_____	_____	_____
Home equity line of credit	_____	_____	_____	_____
Home improvement loan	_____	_____	_____	_____
Installment loan(s)	_____	_____	_____	_____
Passbook or CD loan	_____	_____	_____	_____
Personal loan	_____	_____	_____	_____
Store charge card(s)	_____	_____	_____	_____
Student loan	_____	_____	_____	_____
Other debts (list)	_____	_____	_____	_____
	_____	_____	_____	_____
	_____	_____	_____	_____
	_____	_____	_____	_____

Total of monthly payments $_____

Monthly take-home pay $____ divided by 10 (10%) = $___

divided by 5 (20%) = $___

Figure 9.1 Evaluate Your Credit Status (Continued)

| Take-Home Pay | | Debt Ratios | |
Per Year	Per Month	10%— Safe Level	20%— Danger Level
$12,000	$ 1,000	$100	$200
18,000	1,500	150	300
24,000	2,000	200	400
30,000	2,500	250	500
36,000	3,000	300	600
42,000	3,500	350	700
48,000	4,000	400	800
54,000	4,500	450	900
60,000	5,000	500	1,000
66,000	5,500	550	1,100
72,000	6,000	600	1,200

③ **Avoid Negative Equity**—The purchase of a new car is a major expense and longer term loans are becoming the norm. Longer loans, combined with normal depreciation, can lead to a temporary condition called negative equity (also known as being upside down). This means that the market value of a car is less than its outstanding loan. A car owner would take a loss if the car were sold or stolen during the early months or years of a loan. Shortening the length of a loan will increase monthly payments but reduce the chance of incurring negative equity. For example, a $5,000 loan with a 15 percent APR will cost $242 a month for two years, $173

a month for three years, $139 a month for four years and
$119 a month for five years. The difference in the total
cost of the two-year loan ($5,808) and the five-year loan
($7,140) is $1,332.

④ **Check Your Bills**—Occasionally, a credit card bill
may contain an error. To avoid problems, keep copies of
sales slips and charge account credits and promptly compare figures when bills arrive. If an error is found, you
must notify the card issuer in writing within 60 days of
the date the statement was mailed. The card issuer, in
turn, must investigate the problem within 90 days of
receipt of the complaint. During the investigation, consumers do not have to pay the amount in question.

⑤ **Treat Credit Cards with Care**—Protect credit
cards and account numbers to prevent unauthorized use.
Draw a line through blank spaces above the total on
receipts and rip up or retain the carbons. Report the loss
of a card as soon as possible (many card issuers have
toll-free telephone numbers for this purpose) and follow
up with a letter that includes the account number and
date of loss. Keep a list of credit card numbers and the
address and telephone number of the issuers in your
long-term storage file.

⑥ **Say No to Credit Life Insurance**—Credit life
insurance is often sold by lenders during the loan application process. The purpose of the policy is to repay the
loan balance if a borrower dies. The premium is usually
added to each month's payment. Most experts feel that
the cost of credit life insurance is very high for the
amount of coverage provided. An inexpensive term life

policy is probably a better option (in fact, you may already be adequately covered). Another problem is that credit life is so often discussed in such a way as to imply that it is required. It generally is not and, if it is, borrowers have the option of getting coverage elsewhere or pledging the proceeds of an existing policy.

⑦ **Pledge Collateral**—Many banks make loans secured by assets such as a passbook savings account or CD. The charge is generally two to three percentage points more than the rate earned on savings. Other low-cost sources of funds are cash value life insurance policies (many older policies charge as little as 5 percent) and credit unions.

⑧ **Establish a Credit History**—A credit history is important to establish the creditworthiness of an individual to lenders. It is important for couples to make sure that jointly held credit cards and loans are reported in the name of both spouses. If you have yet to establish a credit history, start by opening a checking and a savings account in your own name, applying for a store charge account or bank card or taking out a small loan. Any charges that are incurred should be repaid promptly.

⑨ **Beware of Cash Advance**—Many consumers are unaware that they pay effective interest rates of 25 to 30 percent or more on credit card cash advances. One reason is that few issuers offer grace periods on cash advances. Many also charge cash advance fees. According to Bankcard Holders of America, consumers who take a $300 advance and are charged a $2.50 fee and one month's interest at 18.5 percent will pay an effective interest rate of 32.94 percent if the advance is repaid 25 days later. Other high-interest loans on an annual basis are those made by pawnshops, rent-to-own stores and electronic tax filers who loan taxpayers their refund.

⑩ **Try Haggling**—In today's highly competitive credit card market, many issuers will waive annual fees or reduce interest rates, upon request, to attract or maintain the business of customers with good credit histories. Just call them and ask them, if necessary, stating that you're willing to defect to another issuer to receive acceptable terms. A 1991 survey of officers of the largest credit-card-issuing banks found that two out of three said they might waive annual fees under certain circumstances, including requests by customers.

Beware Home Equity Loans

One of the fastest growing sources of consumer credit is the home equity credit line. The main reasons for its popularity are relatively low interest rates and tax reform. While the deduction for consumer interest was completely phased out, interest on home equity loans of up to $100,000 is fully deductible.

Lenders are marketing home equity credit lines in a variety of packages. Many of these loans come with variable interest rates tied to a money market index. Some have very low introductory rates and some have fixed rates. Some loans have large one-time up-front fees that are comparable to mortgage closing costs. Others have continuing costs, such as annual fees. Some come with large balloon payments at the end of the loan while others have no balloons but relatively higher monthly payments.

With advertisements galore describing the advantages of home equity loans, it's important to also take a look at their drawbacks. The advisability of a home equity loan depends a great deal on your use of the loan and current level of indebtedness. Using an equity loan to pay off existing debts (especially high-interest credit cards) may be an appropriate use, but only if done so with care. Clearing the slate only to pile up new debt obviously defeats the benefits of this strategy and can lead to trouble as the total amount of debt increases.

Another factor to consider is your income tax filing status. Home equity loans are promoted heavily on the basis of the deductibility of their interest but itemized deductions were claimed on only 28.2 percent of 1991 tax returns. Itemizers and nonitemizers alike may be able to find a more attractive alternative, such as low-rate auto dealer financing programs or a fixed-rate second mortgage.

Remember, home equity lines of credit require that you use your home as collateral for the loan—which will put your home at risk if you cannot make your monthly payments. Those loans that require a balloon payment may necessitate additional borrowing to pay off this obligation. Also, with relatively free access to cash, you may borrow money more freely. If you do decide to apply for a home equity loan, remember that no one loan is suitable for every borrower. The challenge is to sort through the wide range of loan options available and select the one best tailored to your needs.

The Danger Signals of Debt

Many experts have linked overspending to other behaviors or diseases of excess, such as compulsive gambling, overeating and alcoholism. It is estimated that approximately 6 percent of Americans have compulsive spending addictions, with shopping as their drug of choice. The common element of all addictive behaviors is a feeling of being out of control. How do you know when you are in financial trouble? Figure 9.2 provides a list of 30 debt danger signals. If ten or more apply to your household, you are undoubtedly already experiencing problems. If five or more apply, you may be headed for trouble.

Figure 9.2   30 Debt Danger Signals

---

1. Using credit for items that used to be purchased with cash
2. Getting a consolidation loan to pay existing debt
3. Charging more each month than you make in payments
4. Paying only the minimum required payment
5. Juggling rent or mortgage and other large bills to pay debts
6. Rotating bills: paying half of your bills one month and half the next
7. Using checking account overdraft to pay bills
8. Using credit card advances to pay living expenses
9. Writing post-dated checks

Figure 9.2 30 Debt Danger Signals (Continued)

10. Taking out a new loan before an old one is repaid
11. Being chronically overdrawn at the bank
12. Borrowing frequently from friends and relatives
13. Using savings to pay bills that used to be paid by cash or check
14. Depending on overtime or moonlighting to make ends meet
15. Borrowing against life insurance without repayment
16. Being at or near maximum credit limits
17. Being chronically late paying bills
18. Increasing the percentage of take-home pay spent on consumer debt
19. Having late penalties assessed on outstanding debt
20. Receiving calls or overdue notices from creditors
21. Receiving threats of repossession or legal action
22. Negative information contained within a credit report
23. Being denied credit due to negative remarks in a credit report
24. Hiding credit card statements and bills from others
25. Excessive worrying about money and financial distress
26. Having more than seven or eight creditors
27. Owing more than 20 percent of your take-home pay to creditors
28. Committing all of a secondary earner's income to debt
29. Having a total credit balance that rarely decreases
30. Dishonesty with spouse about spending

Getting Help

Consumers have a number of ways to deal with a debt problem. Five are listed below in order of their severity.

The method selected will depend a great deal on a household's debt level and the willingness of its creditors to accept changes in payments.

① **Negotiation with Creditors**—As soon as you experience financial difficulty, contact your creditors before sending in any late payments. Explain your situation and draft a written agreement to reduce monthly payments or extend debt over a longer time period. The sheer number of people who have experienced financial difficulty of late has made creditors more amenable to negotiation if they are contacted early.

② **Credit Counseling**—The Consumer Credit Counseling Service (CCCS) provides professional financial counselors to assist households that have serious debt problems. Each CCCS office is a nonprofit organization affiliated with the National Foundation for Consumer Credit. Counseling sessions are generally free of charge. Consumers who enter a CCCS debt management program agree to send the CCCS a specific amount each week or month toward debt repayment, plus a nominal fee for administrative costs, and to incur no further debt during the duration of the program. CCCS offices are located throughout the United States, providing preventative budget and credit counseling, as well as debt management for those already in financial difficulty. For further information about the CCCS, contact the National Foundation for Consumer Credit, 8611 2nd Avenue, Suite 100, Silver Spring, MD 20910, or call 800-388-CCCS.

③ **Debt Consolidation**—A consolidation loan is a single loan used to pay off a number of prior debts. The payments on the new loan are generally smaller than the total of the payments on prior debts because the repayment schedule is extended. The downside is that consolidation loans are expensive because, first, the term of existing debt is extended, increasing total interest charges. Second, borrowers often end up paying a higher interest rate than they were paying before (e.g., exchanging a 7 percent student loan and a 4.9 percent auto loan for a 14 percent consolidation loan) or, worse yet, consolidating debts, like money owed to doctors, that were previously interest free. Finally, there is the temptation to overspend if monthly payments are reduced and borrowers perceive that they have extra money available. Consolidation loans should be considered only if the rate of interest is *lower* than that on existing debt and if no new debt will be incurred until the loan is repaid.

④ **Chapter 13 Bankruptcy (Reorganization)**—In a Chapter 13 bankruptcy, a plan is proposed and approved by the court to repay all or part of a person's debts within a three-year to five-year period with future earnings. Creditors must receive at least as much as they would have been paid if a debtor had filed Chapter 7. Debtors are allowed to keep their property and make payments to a court-appointed trustee, who reapportions the money to creditors. The difference between income and essential living expenses is the amount proposed for debt repayment. Chapter 13 is best suited to those with steady incomes and equity in secured debts like a home or car.

⑤ **Chapter 7 Bankruptcy (Liquidation)**—This form of bankruptcy is filed by about 70 percent of petitioners and erases all obligations except child support, alimony, student loans and federal and state taxes. Filers must surrender to a bankruptcy trustee all assets that aren't legally exempt but they retain the right to future income. The idea behind exemptions, which include household goods and equity in a home or car, is that debtors retain something with which to start over. Nonexempt assets, if any, are sold by the trustee, with proceeds divided among creditors.

Either form of bankruptcy requires a $120 filing fee and legal fees of generally $350 to $1,000. Most attorneys insist on being paid up front so they don't get added to the list of a debtor's unsecured creditors. Both forms of bankruptcy will be noted in a person's credit record for at least ten years. Opinion is divided over whether this is an overwhelming deterrent to obtaining future lines of credit.

Many people spend more time saving quarters with coupons at the supermarket than they do studying the mortgages, loans and credit cards into which they will pour thousands of dollars over the years. This is a costly mistake. Credit is a convenience that allows consumers to buy now and pay later but it does not come cheaply. A common financial error is greater concern with the size of monthly payments than with the total cost of a loan. Borrowers learn that they can carry a $1,000 debt for less than $30 a month, which becomes $2,000 for less than $60, then $5,000 for less than $150. Then a crisis occurs. According to a recent survey by the National Foundation for Consumer Credit, people seek debt counseling for the following reasons: poor money management (45 percent), unemployment (28 percent), divorce (10 percent), medical problems and disability (8 percent), substance abuse (1 percent) and other reasons (8 percent).

Wise use of credit can save a lot of unnecessary worry, embarrassment and expense. It also increases the amount of income available for saving. Many Americans went on a spending spree during the 1980s, racking up bills on their credit cards for which they are still paying. This chapter has described dozens of ways to stay out of debt or dig out from under. Debt doesn't have to be a permanent condition. Taking control with a plan to reduce it is the key to success.

10

Am I Covered? How To Get the Best Insurance at the Lowest Cost

Risk is unavoidable. Every day, people face events and engage in activities that could potentially erase both their accumulated savings and their prospects for achieving financial independence. Risk can be handled in a variety of ways. One way is to simply avoid certain risks, such as smoking, skiing, high diving or driving in a blinding snow storm. You can also choose to incur a risk but take steps to reduce the impact of a potential loss. Wearing seat belts or safety equipment, driving only when alert and sober and installing smoke detectors in your home are common examples.

Some risks are so potentially large and unpredictable that they cannot be handled personally—premature death, long-term disability, large medical expenses, liability and the total destruction of your home, for example. That is why insurance markets exist: for the transfer of these risks to a third party, an insurance company. Establishing and maintaining a sound insurance program can limit the financial impact of devastating losses.

A basic definition of insurance is the payment of a relatively small known cost, the premium, in exchange for coverage against a larger, uncertain loss. Death, illness or accident, legal liability and property loss are the major risks that most families face. The wisest use of insurance premium dollars is to maximize protection against risks with the greatest potential for financial loss. This is called the large-loss principle. The potential magnitude of a loss, rather than its frequency, should be of prime concern.

Consider a 30-year-old worker earning $35,000 annually who becomes fully disabled for life. Ignoring future cost-of-living salary adjustments and possible promotions he or she could have earned, more than $1 million of potential wages would be lost without disability insurance. Another large risk is liability for damages inflicted on others. Most court-awarded settlements today start in the six-figure range and multimillion-dollar judgments are not unheard of.

The Risk of Premature Death

If the loss of a person's income or services (e.g., homemaking tasks and child care) would result in a reduced standard of living, life insurance should be purchased. The more income a person provides, the more insurance he or she needs, unless that person owns substantial assets that can be converted to cash (e.g., real estate, securities, etc.). Most two-paycheck families need less life insurance than single-earner families because the surviving spouse also has an income. This reduces the need for "widow's" or "widower's" income during the years preceding the survivor's retirement, when Social Security payments to children cease.

The purpose of life insurance is to provide an instant estate or a stream of income for dependents in the event of a wage earner's death. Insurance proceeds are often used initially to pay everyday living costs, medical and funeral expenses and perhaps estate taxes. Many people forget this principle when they purchase life insurance on their children. Unless children are successful models or actors, their death, while devastating emotionally, will not generally result in severe financial loss. The insurance premiums spent on children's policies should be used instead to strengthen their parents' coverage.

Before looking at any specific types of policies, determine how much coverage you need. The best way to do this is with a worksheet or computer program designed to take into account future income needs and funds already available to a surviving spouse or surviving children. This method provides a much more accurate estimate than simplistic rules of thumb, such as multiplying income by four or five. Two-income households should purchase coverage proportionate to each spouse's contribution to household income, and single persons without dependents may not need life insurance at all.

Many insurance agents suggest buying enough life insurance to allow dependents to invest the proceeds of a policy and live off the income. With an 8 percent return, a $150,000 policy would produce only $12,000 of annual income. Therefore, this strategy is often not affordable for middle-income households. A wage earner providing $30,000 after taxes would need almost $400,000 of coverage to protect dependents without spending any face value.

Young families can generally purchase the most coverage for the least cost with term insurance. Term insurance is protection for a specific period of time or term, usually one, five or ten years. It pays proceeds only if a policyholder dies during the term, and it builds up no cash value. Premiums increase each time the policy is renewed because the insured has aged.

It is important to know your life insurance needs before any purchase and to buy only what you need and can afford. Beware, also, of life insurance fads. The hot product of the late 1980s, single-premium cash value policies, requires a lump-sum premium of at least $5,000. Depending on a policyholder's age, a certain amount of insurance protection is provided. A 35-year-old male purchasing a $25,000 single-premium policy might receive a death benefit of slightly more than $80,000. This is not a lot of insurance for a person with several dependents and, also, many people would not have such a large lump sum available.

Protecting Your Earning Power

One of the most overlooked facets of family financial planning is disability insurance, also known as income continuation protection. Disability insurance covers income losses when you're unable to work. Many people who have individual life and health policies, or have these benefits provided by their employer, neglect to consider the risk of loss of income due to accident or illness. Fewer than 25 percent of Americans are covered for this risk.

When sick days (if you even have them) run out, it is often difficult to pay ongoing expenses (e.g., mortgage, utilities, food), not to mention accumulating medical bills. About 48 percent of all mortgage foreclosures are due to disability, compared to only 3 percent due to death. A 32-year-old is more than three times as likely to suffer a disability of 90 days or more than to die and one-third of all workers will become disabled for more than 60 days before reaching age 65.

When considering disability insurance, first find out what benefits, if any, are provided by your employer. Most employer-provided disability benefits last two years or less and may replace only a small percentage of income. They are better than nothing, however, and plan documents need to be studied carefully. Workers in several states also have another short-term source of funds—temporary disability benefits funded by payroll deduction.

If you have little or no coverage through your employer, you will need to contact an insurance agent for individual coverage. Some factors to consider are the following:

① **Maximum Benefit Period**—This is the period of time that benefits will be paid to a disabled person. The longer this period, the greater the coverage (and the cost) for the insured. It is recommended that the benefit period extend until retirement age.

② **Elimination (Waiting) Period**—This is the period of time (e.g., 90 days) that must elapse after a covered disability starts before benefits begin. Generally, the longer the elimination period, the lower the premium for a given amount of coverage.

③ **Definition of Disability**—This determines when a person is considered disabled for purposes of collecting benefits. The best policies define disability as being unable to perform your present job, while others say you're not disabled unless you can perform no job whatsoever.

The best policies cover disability from either an accident or an illness to age 65, define disability as the inability to engage in any and every duty pertaining to your regular occupation and are noncancelable or guaranteed renewable.

Protecting Your Property

Homeowners insurance protects against damage to your home and personal property. The amount of insurance carried on a dwelling is the most important figure because other property loss limits are usually stated as a percentage of it. Homeowners insurance also protects against liability for another person's injury or damage to that person's property. For instance if your dog bites a jogger or a limb from your tree damages a neighbor's car, the insurance company will generally pay for damages up to the limits of the policy.

Most insurers require that a home be insured for at least 80 percent of its replacement cost for full coverage. Replacement cost is the amount you would have to spend today to rebuild a home, excluding the value of its land and foundation. The 80 percent figure represents the minimum amount required to receive full payment for a *partial* loss. Suppose your home has a replacement cost of $150,000 and you insure it for the required 80 percent, or $120,000. If you incur a $20,000 loss, you will receive full payment. To determine the replacement cost of your home, request a copy of your mortgage lender's appraisal or ask a licensed property and casualty agent to calculate it for you. The standard method of determining replacement cost is to multiply local construction costs per square foot by the number of square feet in your home.

You must insure your home for 100 percent of its replacement cost to receive full payment if it is *totally* destroyed. If your home burns to the ground, you can be reimbursed only up to the face value of your policy. If you're insured for $120,000, for example, and rebuilding your home costs $150,000, you must pay the difference. An insurance company is never required to pay more for a loss than the amount of insurance carried.

As a general rule, the contents of a home are insured for no more than half of the coverage on the home. If personal possessions are lost or damaged, standard actual cash value policies reimburse the current replacement cost minus depreciation. A better choice is to add a replacement cost endorsement to your policy. This will replace lost or damaged property at current market prices up to a limit specified in the policy. If you own expensive items, such as jewelry or silver coins, a floater policy to insure their full value is advisable.

Never let a mortgage lender mislead you into thinking that you need only insure for the amount of your loan. This could leave you dangerously underinsured. Also, be sure to review your homeowners policy frequently. Although many policies today have a clause that automatically increases coverage to adjust for inflation, you should still review your coverage to make sure that it is in line with local building costs.

Liability Insurance

You are liable for damages if you are found by a court to be the cause of another person's injury or loss of life or property. Liability cases clog our nation's court system and can result in substantial loss to persons who are not properly insured.

Most people have some liability insurance as part of their automobile policy and homeowners or renters insurance. Homeowners policies contain general liability insurance for a broad range of occurrences, excluding auto accidents, while automobile insurance provides coverage if one is found liable as a result of the use of his or her car.

Auto and homeowners policies, however, provide liability coverage only up to a specified maximum amount, such as $100,000 or $300,000. Because we live in a litigious society, many financial experts feel that this is not enough. Umbrella policies, also known as excess liability, supplement auto and homeowners insurance and cover claims that exceed the limits of these policies. They generally have a face value of at least $1 million and cost about $150 a year.

Umbrella liability policies also usually cover liability for charges of slander or libel. Because they pick up where other coverage ends, insurers require a certain amount (e.g., $300,000) of underlying homeowners and automobile insurance as deductibles for the policy.

The increasing tendency for Americans to sue whenever they feel wronged necessitates having adequate liability insurance for a financially secure future. The low cost of umbrella liability coverage—less than $3 a week—makes it a cost-effective way to cover the risk of having to pay a six-figure or seven-figure judgment.

Selecting a Policy

Insurance companies are a plentiful lot. Some specialize in life and health insurance, some specialize in property and casualty insurance and others offer all of the above. If you're thinking about buying a new insurance policy, consider the following:

① **Check the reputation of an insurance company** through one or more of the five rating firms

(A.M. Best, Standard & Poor's, Moody's, Weiss Research and Duff & Phelps), your state insurance department or a local better business bureau. You can find rating reports in most public libraries. These publications contain information on insurance companies and use a rating scale similar to school grades (A+, A, B+, B, etc.).

② **Make sure that an insurance company and agent are licensed to sell in your state** (a business card is not a license). Find out how long a company and an agent have been in business.

③ **Find out how quickly claims are settled.** Start by consulting *Consumer Reports*, which periodically reviews insurance company performance. When comparing insurers' complaint experience, also compare their respective numbers of contracts in force.

④ **Don't be fooled by official-sounding titles** (e.g., Veterans Insurance Policy, Armed Forces Insurance, etc.) in mail-order or other types of insurance advertisements. If someone tells you that an insurance policy is endorsed by a government agency, don't believe it. The government doesn't do this.

⑤ **Remember, it is the policy itself, not what a salesperson says, that spells out the obligations of an insurance company.** An insurance policy is a legal contract. Any statement made by an agent that is not contained in the contract is not binding on the company.

⑥ **Don't be embarrassed to ask questions.** Persist until all your questions are answered and you understand what is and is not covered. Check out a policy thoroughly. You have too much at stake not to do so. The wrong insurance can be as dangerous as no insurance at all.

⑦ **Make sure you know what an insurance company *won't* cover.** Deductibles, coinsurance, coordination of benefits with other policies and policy limits (e.g., $500 for jewelry) will reduce the amount of coverage provided. Study carefully a policy's exclusions. Some exclusions (e.g., nuclear war, workers'-compensation-covered accidents) are fairly standard. Others vary from policy to policy.

⑧ **Check the specifics of your health insurance policies.** These are often overlooked because many people are covered as part of an employee group plan. Check the amount of coverage on your group plan, especially the maximum limit on major medical. A $250,000 *family lifetime limit* is poor in light of current medical costs. A $1 million dollar *annual limit per person* is much better.

⑨ **Also examine a policy *after* you buy it to make sure it matches your application and the coverage requested.** Conditions may have changed as a result of medical tests or the information contained within your application.

Figure 10.1 provides a list of common insurance errors to avoid.

Figure 10.1   Common Insurance Errors

1. Purchasing too much insurance, not enough insurance or the wrong type of insurance
2. Purchasing an insurance policy that duplicates all or part of the coverage of an existing policy
3. Failing to keep adequate insurance records
4. Failing to review insurance coverage periodically, especially during major life changes (e.g., marriage)
5. Failing to discontinue coverage when it's no longer needed or is no longer cost-efficient
6. Covering minor risks (e.g., a fender-bender) while major risks (e.g., liability) are underinsured
7. Failing to update coverage to keep pace with inflation
8. Purchasing insurance that covers just one risk (e.g., cancer)
9. Failing to consider insurance protection as part of an overall financial plan
10. Failing to read an insurance policy thoroughly and ask questions, if necessary
11. Dealing with agents who fail to fully explain a policy
12. Failing to inform close family members about insurance coverage and the location of policies
13. Switching or cancelling policies indiscriminately
14. Cancelling an existing policy before a new policy is officially approved
15. Failing to check the rating of an insurance company before purchasing a policy
16. Failing to comparison-shop for insurance coverage
17. Paying increased administrative costs (e.g., commissions) by purchasing multiple policies
18. Failing to inquire about insurance policy discounts
19. Purchasing inadedquate life insurance on household wage earners

Figure 10.1 Common Insurance Errors (Continued)

20. Purchasing life insurance on a child
21. Purchasing credit life insurance when borrowing money
22. Buying life insurance primarily as an investment
23. Buying a health insurance policy that pays a set amount (e.g., $50) per day for hospital care instead of a fixed percentage (e.g., 80 percent) of total expenses
24. Purchasing health insurance with a lifetime limit of $250,000 or less
25. Failing to continue group health insurance or purchase an individual policy when employment ceases
26. Lacking disability insurance, if employed, or having coverage that replaces less than 60 percent of income
27. Failing to increase disability insurance as household income increases
28. Failing to purchase a homeowners insurance policy endorsement to cover valuables (e.g., art, antiques, jewelry) for their entire appraised value
29. Failing to insure for the business use of a home
30. Lacking a replacement cost endorsement for personal property in a homeowners insurance policy
31. Obtaining a dwelling coverage on a homeowners policy of less than 80 percent of replacement cost (the cost of rebuilding)
32. Lacking property damage and liability coverage for loss caused by tenants
33. Having low bodily injury liability and property damage limits on car insurance
34. Having collision and comprehensive coverage on older cars
35. Lacking umbrella liability insurance if assets (including home) total more than $300,000

Maximizing Insurance Protection
on a Shoestring

The average household spends more than $3,000 a year for property, health, life and disability insurance. Below is a list of ten proven ways to reduce premiums without sacrificing essential coverage:

① **Raise Deductibles**—Covering small losses instead of large ones is a poor use of insurance dollars. A deductible means that you are insuring yourself in the event of a small loss and letting an insurance company cover the risk of a large loss. Because small losses are more frequent than large losses, larger deductibles will reduce your premium. Of course, it's also important to establish an adequate emergency fund to cover such losses should they occur.

② **Use Discounts**—Insurance discounts vary from company to company. Examples include lower life insurance premiums for nonsmokers and the physically fit, lower homeowners insurance premiums for households with smoke detectors or alarm systems and auto insurance rate reductions for multiple-car owners, persons who drive less than three to five miles to work and compact-car owners. Make sure you receive any discounts that you're entitled to.

③ **Pay Premiums Less Often**—Paying premiums in installments can add 5 to 10 percent to the cost of a policy. The more frequently payments are made, the greater the amount of paperwork that must be completed by an insurance company. Annual or semi-annual payments reduce this cost and insurance companies generally pass along these savings in the form of lower premiums.

④ **Buy Group Insurance**—Group policies are generally less expensive than individual policies because the insurance company has only one contract to administer. A reduction in the number of policies means reduced administrative costs and lower premiums. In many cases, too, coverage is paid for, entirely or in part, by employers. If your job does not provide group coverage, see if you can qualify through a union or professional organization.

⑤ **Cut Administrative Costs**—If you need, say, $200,000 in life insurance, don't buy four $50,000 policies. Having one policy reduces administrative costs for the insurance company and premium costs for the consumer.

⑥ **Eliminate the Middleman**—In some cases, insurance can be purchased directly from an insurance company rather than through an agent, thereby eliminating commission costs. This should be done only when you know exactly what type of policy you want and when you've checked on the reputation and financial strength of the insurer.

⑦ **Avoid Narrowly Defined Coverage**—Insurance policies that cover only one type of risk (e.g., cancer, accidents) often appear inexpensive at first glance. The problem, of course, is that their risk coverage is so narrow. Relatively few benefits are paid out as a percentage of premiums paid in and, in addition, many such policies duplicate existing coverage. Moreover, the needs of dependents are the same no matter how a wage earner dies so there is absolutely no reason why one potential cause of death should receive special coverage. Other examples of questionable coverage are credit life insurance and flight insurance.

⑧ **Shop Around**—Not only do policies differ from insurer to insurer but so do premiums and discounts for similar coverage. The only way to find the best buy is to shop around and try to get quotes for the same type and amount of coverage. The companies you select should be financially stable, have a good track record for handling claims and charge competitive premiums.

⑨ **Drop the Unnecessary**—Don't pay for insurance you no longer need. Examples include life insurance after dependents are grown, collision and comprehensive on older vehicles and duplicate benefits provided, for a fee, to spouses in two-paycheck households.

⑩ **Review and Revise**—Just as some insurance coverage can be reduced as circumstances change, other policies may need to be strengthened. Examples include disability income protection, as salaries rise with inflation, and homeowners insurance, to keep pace with rising property values. In addition, changes in the insurance industry may prompt a policy revision. Premiums for term life insurance and disability insurance for women were reduced significantly during the 1980s.

The savings from policies that are dropped or exchanged can be used to offset the higher cost of increased coverage elsewhere.

When purchasing insurance, it's important to weigh the risk of potentially devastating losses against the cost of premiums. Cutting coverage in the wrong places to save money can backfire and cost a lot more over time. Insurance should be maximized on catastrophic losses that can't possibly be paid out of pocket. While it won't reduce your risk of incurring a loss, insurance will reduce the serious after-effects on your finances, leaving more money available to save.

11

Enough Is Enough—50 Ways To Reduce Your Income Tax

Unless you're reading this book on or about April 15th, income taxes are probably the last thing on your mind. They shouldn't be! Federal and state taxes become a closed chapter on December 31st of each year. After that, you can do little between January 1st and April 15th that will make a difference in the amount of tax you pay. One exception is a fully or partially deductible individual retirement account (IRA) contribution, which can be made until April 15th of the year following the one for which taxes are due.

Serious tax planning should begin no later than May or June, thereby providing at least six months to make changes that can save money. Unfortunately, Congress has not made tax planning easy. During the past 20 years, more than a dozen tax laws were passed, each with a new interpretation of existing regulations and, in many cases, new tax forms to decipher and file. Many taxpayers have subsequently turned to tax preparers for assistance. In 1993, about half of the 114.9 million individual tax returns the IRS received were completed by paid preparers.

Whether you hire someone to do your taxes or you do your own, if recent tax law changes haven't altered your behavior, you're probably doing something wrong. Sweeping changes in itemized deductions and the tax ramifications of consumer purchases and investments have affected just about everyone. If you're buying a car, refinancing a mortgage, charging purchases on a credit card or saving for retirement or a child's college education, the rules of the game keep changing. Below is a list of 50 tax-saving strategies to consider:

Recordkeeping

1. Keep good records. This will help ensure maximum use of tax deductions and credits and provide evidence in the event of an audit. Think taxes every time you make a major financial transaction (e.g., home sale, stock purchase, car loan).

2. Keep day-to-day records of mileage or car expenses for business, charitable and medical purposes. Keep a log or calendar in your car to record mileage figures and destinations as you travel.

Investing

3. If your marginal tax bracket warrants it, consider investing in municipal bonds, municipal bond unit trusts, tax-exempt mutual funds or tax-exempt money

market funds. To determine whether a *taxable* or *tax-exempt* product is best, shop around. Then do some math. Divide the available tax-exempt rate by 1 minus your marginal tax bracket. This gives you its taxable equivalent. Unless you can find a taxable investment consistent with your risk tolerance level, paying a higher return, buy a tax-exempt one. Let's assume you're in the 28 percent marginal tax bracket. If a tax-exempt investment yields 7 percent, it is equivalent to a 9.72 percent taxable investment: 7 divided by .72 (1 −.28) equals 9.72. In the 15 percent bracket, a 7 percent tax-exempt investment is equivalent to 8.24 percent: 7 divided by .85 (1 −.15) equals 8.24.

4. Plan your investment strategies with taxes in mind. Compute paper gains and losses several times a year to see where you stand. Use capital losses to offset capital gains. Remember, too, that mutual fund family transfers (e.g., a stock mutual fund to a money market mutual fund) are taxable events.

5. Save all stock and mutual fund dividend reinvestment and trade confirmation statements to determine your basis for capital-gain-reporting purposes. Tax basis is the initial purchase price of a security plus additional purchases and reinvested dividends and capital gains that accrue over the years.

6. If you have children younger than age 14 with more than $1,200 of *unearned* income, choose investments

that avoid the "kiddie tax." This is where children must pay taxes at their parents' generally higher rate. Shift funds into municipal bonds or bond funds, U.S. savings bonds to be redeemed after age 14, annuities, growth stocks or growth/equity-type mutual funds that pay small dividends. After a child turns 14, all income will be taxed at his or her own rate, which is usually 15 percent.

7. If you still have passive losses from a limited partnership, which were phased out as a tax deduction years ago, invest in unleveraged income limited partnerships to produce offsetting passive income.

8. Invest in tax-deferred U.S. savings bonds. You pay no federal tax until the bonds mature and no state tax. Since 1990, interest earned on EE savings bonds is exempt from federal taxes if the bonds are used to pay for a child's college education. To qualify, bonds must be bought in a parent's name (and not his or her child's) by a purchaser at least 24 years of age whose income does not exceed certain limits, which are adjusted annually for inflation. The 1994 limits at which the EE bond tax exemption is fully phased out are $56,200 for singles and $91,850 for joint filers.

9. Invest in U.S. Treasury securities for a competitive rate of return free from state and local income taxes. You can purchase Treasury bills, notes or bonds directly from a Federal Reserve Bank or pay a $25 to $50 commission and buy them at a bank or brokerage firm.

10. Consider purchasing a cash value life insurance policy (e.g., whole life, universal life) that apportions premium payments among an insurance component and a savings component. The savings portion grows tax deferred. Shop around for policies with low fees, high ratings and high guaranteed rates of return.

11. When you want to avoid taxation on investment interest in a particular year, buy products like Treasury bills and certificates of deposit (CDs) with maturity dates of up to a year (or more) away. Be sure to specify that interest earned should be paid at maturity.

Borrowing Money

12. Pay off debts as soon as possible. Since 1991, consumer interest on credit card bills, bank loans and other nonmortgage debt has not been deductible.

13. Very carefully consider using home equity loans if you need to borrow money. If you can itemize, interest on loans of up to $100,000 is deductible. Be aware, however, that overborrowing can cost you your home and that 15-year or 20-year repayment schedules and variable interest rates can be costly. Shop around and proceed with caution.

Deductions

14. Time your deductions. Lump them together in one year to take advantage of itemizing if they are close

to the standard deduction amount. The standard deductions for 1994 are $3,800 for singles, $5,600 for heads of household, $6,350 for married couples filing jointly and $3,175 for separately filing married persons.

15. Make an extra month's mortgage payment to increase the amount of interest you can deduct for a given tax year. Sending in January's payment before Christmas should result in interest being credited before year's end.

16. Try to reduce your adjusted gross income (AGI). This will qualify you for larger medical and miscellaneous itemized deductions (because they must exceed a percentage of AGI) and, perhaps, an IRA deduction. Alimony payments and Keogh and salary reduction plan contributions (e.g., 401(k) and 403(b) plans) are examples of ways to reduce AGI.

17. Mileage from a job to school or a job to another job is deductible. Commuting from home to a job is not.

18. Gambling losses are allowed to the extent of winnings—but only if you itemize deductions. You do *not* have to meet the cap of 2 percent of AGI for miscellaneous itemized deductions. Save your receipts, where possible, and keep a diary to document the remainder of your losing bets.

19. Consider donating appreciated property (e.g., real estate, stock, antiques) to charity in lieu of cash. This way, you avoid the capital gains tax that otherwise must be paid upon the sale of assets.

20. Remember, deductible *business* meal expenses include the tip but only 50 percent of the total cost is deductible, down from 80 percent in 1993 and prior years. For example, for a $35 business dinner with a $5 tip, $20 is deductible ($40 × .50). Be sure to keep the receipt and record the nature of the business transacted.

21. Deduct the cost of attending conventions or seminars that advance your business interests or professional expertise. Unless you're a business owner, however, these costs must exceed 2 percent of your AGI to be deductible as a miscellaneous itemized deduction. Also, the total of all your itemized deductions must exceed the standard deduction.

22. Consider starting a secondary or a consulting business to deduct expenses that are limited or denied in your capacity as an employee. You could then also begin a Keogh plan. Be sure, however, that the business shows a profit in three out of five consecutive years or it could be declared a hobby and its deductions disallowed.

23. If you own your own business, hire your spouse for a reasonable amount of compensation and place all or part of the salary in an IRA.

24. You can also hire your children to work in a family-owned business. As long as the wages paid are reasonable, they are deductible as a business expense. Children with little or no interest income and less than $3,000 a year in wages should see minor tax consequences as a result of this strategy.

25. The standard mileage rate for business use of a car was increased in 1994 to 29 cents per mile. If your employer's reimbursement is less than that, deduct the difference. For instance, if you drive 10,000 miles and are reimbursed only 22 cents a mile, you are entitled to a deduction of $700: 10,000 times 7 cents.

26. Consider becoming a landlord if your AGI is less than $100,000. You can use losses, including depreciation, to offset up to $25,000 of income from other sources. The tax break for landlords phases out for those with an AGI exceeding $100,000 and is eliminated at AGI levels of $150,000 and above.

Homeownership

27. Owning your own home continues to be one of the best tax shelters available. Mortgage interest and property taxes on a first and second home are fully deductible if you can itemize.

28. Deduct points, also known as loan origination fees, paid to purchase or refinance a home. A point is a prepayment of interest remitted at or before closing. Points can be deducted in full on a loan for a new home but must be amortized over the life of the loan for a refinanced home (e.g., $3,000 in points divided by 30 years equals $100 per year). If the loan is paid off before its maturity, however, the unamortized points can be completely deducted at that time.

29. As soon as you purchase a new home, begin saving all records pertaining to its closing costs and capital

improvements. You'll need them to determine your basis in the property when it's sold. Tax basis is the purchase price of a home plus certain acquisition costs paid at closing (e.g., title search, survey, attorney fees) plus capital improvements made over the course of home ownership (e.g., deck, fireplace, carpeting, garage door opener, landscaping). The higher your basis, the lower your capital gain and potential tax liability will be.

30. Postpone the taxes owed on profit from the sale of a principal residence by buying, within two years, a new home that costs as much or more than the home that was sold.

31. Take advantage of the once-in-a-lifetime election to exclude up to $125,000 of taxable gain on a personal residence. Persons older than age 55, or couples with at least one spouse older than age 55, who have lived in their home for at least three of the five years prior to its sale are eligible for an exclusion from tax of up to $125,000 of their capital gain.

32. If you own a vacation home, stay in it more than 14 days a year or 10 percent of the time the home is in use by others. That way, you'll be legally able to call it a second residence and deduct all of the mortgage interest and property taxes incurred.

33. Consider refinancing your home mortgage if the interest is currently insufficient to allow itemization of deductions and you can afford the monthly payments (see Chapter 4 for details).

Retirement Planning

34. Open an IRA if you're younger than age 70½ and have earned income. The deduction for an IRA contribution depends on your AGI and whether you (or your spouse, if married) have an employer retirement plan. The law retains a *full* deduction for persons not covered by an employer retirement plan (regardless of income), individuals with AGIs of less than $25,000 and jointly filing couples with AGIs of less than $40,000. Individuals with AGIs of up to $35,000 and couples who earn up to $50,000 get a *partial* deduction. Taxpayers with employer plans and incomes exceeding the cut-off amounts can contribute up to $2,000 annually and the earnings on their IRAs accumulate tax deferred. They are not allowed to deduct their annual contributions, however.

35. If you have a nondeductible IRA and file tax form #8606, save a copy of it and the #1040 form with which it was filed until you've withdrawn all your funds, which could mean the rest of your life. In order to determine what part of future IRA distributions is taxable, you'll need good records of your deductible and nondeductible contributions and earnings over the years.

36. Use alimony payments as income for an IRA contribution if you're divorced and can afford it.

37. If you're self-employed, either as a primary occupation or as a sideline, open a Keogh (HR-10) account.

The amount contributed to this retirement savings program is deductible from gross income. Self-employment income includes net income from a sole proprietorship or partnership, income earned as an independent contractor, consulting fees, director's fees and royalties from the sale of books. The most common type of Keogh account, the defined contribution plan, has a generous annual contribution limit of the lesser of 25 percent of net earnings or $30,000.

38. Corporate employees with access to a 401(k) plan can reduce their salary by payroll deduction up to $9,240 in 1994 to save for retirement and lower their tax bill at the same time. Because contributions are made with *before-tax dollars*, both the amount you reduce your salary by and its earnings are tax deferred. If you earn $30,000 and defer $3,000, for instance, you pay federal income tax on only $27,000.

39. Two other types of employer-sponsored retirement savings plans can also reduce taxes: 403(b) plans for employees of schools, colleges and nonprofit organizations and Section 457 deferred compensation plans for county and municipal government workers. They also have the advantage of allowing before-tax dollars to be set aside for retirement, up to $9,500 for 403(b) plans and a $7,500 maximum for Section 457 plans.

40. Consider purchasing an annuity to build assets on a tax-deferred basis. An annuity is a contract issued by

a life insurance company that guarantees periodic payments for life or a certain period in exchange for either a lump-sum payment or a series of payments made by the purchaser. Contact an insurance agent or a brokerage firm for details. The minimum lump sum needed to invest is usually $5,000.

41. If you leave a job and receive a lump-sum distribution from a qualified pension or profit-sharing plan, establish a rollover IRA to continue deferring tax until you need the money. To avoid having 20 percent withheld for taxes, request that your former employer transfer the funds directly to this account.

42. Seek professional advice when you retire with a lump-sum pension distribution. The way you elect to receive the money can save thousands of dollars in taxes. If you were age 50 or older by January 1, 1986, you are still eligible to use the ten-year, forward-averaging technique. This taxes you as if you earned the lump sum over ten years, thereby reducing your tax liability.

Miscellaneous

43. Don't mistakenly report income that's not taxable. Some examples are child support, gifts, inheritances and damages received from a personal injury lawsuit.

44. If you overlooked a money-saving deduction or credit on a prior year's tax return, request a copy of form #1040X and file an amended return. You have

three years from the due date of the original return to amend it.

45. Know your marginal tax bracket, the percentage you pay in taxes on the last dollar of income you earn. Currently, five federal marginal tax brackets exist: 15 percent, 28 percent, 31 percent, 36 percent and 39.6 percent. The 1994 taxable income breakpoints for the three most common brackets are provided in Figure 11.1.

46. Make sure that adequate support payments are made for any person claimed as an exemption on a tax return. You must pay at least one-half of the support of each dependent.

Figure 11.1 Tax Rate Schedules for 1994

Filing Status	Taxable Income	Effective Rate
Married, filing jointly	$ 0–$38,000	15%
	38,001– 91,850	28%
	91,851–140,000	31%
Head of household	$ 0–$30,500	15%
	30,501– 78,700	28%
	78,701–127,500	31%
Single	$ 0–$22,750	15%
	22,751– 55,100	28%
	55,101–115,000	31%
Married, filing separately	$ 0–$19,000	15%
	19,001– 45,925	28%
	45,926– 70,000	31%

47. Compute the correct number of withholding allowances for your household on form W-4 once a year or more often if financial circumstances change. If less than 90 percent of your tax liability is withheld, you could owe a penalty. Don't have your employer overwithhold taxes, either. Think about it. Would you lend money interest free to a casual acquaintance or coworker? Probably not. And if you did, you would charge that person a market-based rate so you could recoup the loss of interest on the money you've lent. If you wouldn't give someone you know an interest-free loan, why give the government one?

48. Consider preparing a mid-year tax mock-up each year (around July) to make sure tax withholding is in line with anticipated income and deductions. Make withholding changes as needed.

49. If you're confused about tax rules and regulations or how to fill out a tax form that you've never used before, seek professional help. You'll need to pull together your own records, however, to get maximum benefit from a paid preparer's expertise.

50. Read the financial press to become familiar with ever-changing tax laws and their ramifications. Attend seminars on personal finance offered by investment firms, Cooperative Extension offices (a nationwide network of adult education programs affiliated with state land-grant universities), colleges or adult schools. Request IRS publication #17, "Your Income Tax," each year to familiarize your-

self with current tax regulations and filing requirements.

The income tax structure of the United States is complex and ever-changing. Small wonder. It's been developing in piecemeal fashion since 1913, not only as a way
to raise revenue for government services but also to
encourage and reward certain behaviors (e.g., home ownership, saving for retirement) deemed important and
politically desirable at the time legislation is passed.

The taxes paid by Americans vary not only due to dif-
ferences in income and household composition but also
as a result of decisions made about borrowing, spending,
saving and investing money. Most people can control, at
least to some extent, the amount of income tax they owe.
The keys to successfully lowering your tax bill are a
thorough understanding of current tax laws and sufficient
time to make changes that reduce taxable income.

Actions taken to reduce taxes generally lead to a
greater accumulation of savings over time because tax-
deferred investments far exceed their taxable counterparts, especially if left to grow undisturbed for long periods
of time. Consider a taxpayer in the 28 percent marginal
tax bracket who saves $2,000 annually for 30 years and
earns a 10 percent annual return. In an IRA or a before-
tax-dollar employer retirement savings plan, this would
grow to $361,887. If the same money were placed in a
taxable investment, only $209,960 would accumulate, a
$150,000 difference.

12

While There's Still Time— Saving for a Comfortable Retirement

It's tough enough to plan your finances day to day, let alone project 10 to 40 years into the future. Long-term goals like a comfortable retirement keep preretirement planning on the back burner. Many people find themselves living on less money than desired or working longer than expected because their retirement saving was delayed.

If you haven't started saving for retirement, now is the time. The more sources of income you have and the earlier you start saving, the more comfortable your retirement is likely to be. Exactly how much money will you need to retire comfortably? There is no easy answer because a lot depends on your lifestyle, expectations and goals. Do you plan to travel, for example, or sell your home and move to a less expensive region of the country? Other factors to consider include the age at which you retire, your life expectancy (about which you need to make some assumptions), the type and amount of employer benefits, if any, and the amount and growth rate of existing savings.

Once these factors are identified, the amount of additional money needed can be calculated mathematically using time value of money multipliers (see Figure 12.1). Plans can then be made to save the required amount. It is absolutely essential that a dollar figure be attached to this goal or it will remain vague and unaccomplished.

Figure 12.1   20 Steps to Retirement Income Planning

1. **Current annual income** (if married, use your combined income)		_____ $/yr.
2. **Retirement income goal** (use at least 60 percent of the amount on line 1)		_____ $/yr.

	Husband	Wife
3. Current age	_____	_____
4. Life expectancy (see table below)	_____	_____

Average Life Expectancy at Given Ages*

Current Age	Male	Female
30	80	85
35	80	85
40	80	85
45	81	85
50	81	85
55	82	86
60	83	86
65	84	87
70	85	88
75	87	89

Figure 12.1   20 Steps to Retirement Income Planning (Continued)

*You'll have to make some assumptions here. You may want to assume more years than your actual life expectancy to compensate for inflationary periods or to ensure that you won't outlive your money. If you are married, use the *higher* life expectancy, whether yours or your spouse's, in your calculations.

	Husband	Wife
5. Age at which you plan to retire	_____	_____
6. Number of years in retirement (subtract line 5 from line 4)	_____	_____
7. Number of years left to save for retirement (subtract line 3 from line 5)	_____	_____

8. Estimated Social Security benefits $_____/yr. $_____/yr.

Total: $_____/yr.

9. Estimated pension benefits	Husband	Wife
Current job	$_____/yr.	$_____/yr.
Previous job #1	$_____/yr.	$_____/yr.
Previous job #2	$_____/yr.	$_____/yr.
Previous job #3	$_____/yr.	$_____/yr.

Total: $_____/yr.

10. Estimated total of Social Security and pension benefits (add line 8 and line 9) $_____

11. Additional income needed for retirement (subtract line 10 from line 2) $_____

Figure 12.1   20 Steps to Retirement Income Planning (Continued)

12. **Amount needed to save
    in today's dollars** (multiply
    line 11 by the multiplier in
    Column A that corresponds to
    the number of years in retire-
    ment, shown on line 6) $_____

13. **Amount you've saved already   Husband   Wife**
    a) IRAs $_____ $_____

    b) Salary reduction plans
       (e.g., 401(k)s and 403(b)s) $_____ $_____

    c) Profit-sharing, stock bonus
       and thrift plans $_____ $_____

    d) Invested assets (e.g., bonds,
       stock, annuities, mutual
       funds, CDs) $_____ $_____

    e) Equity in home or other
       real estate (only if you plan
       to sell the property and use
       the proceeds) $_____ $_____

    f) Other assets or property $_____ $_____

                                    Total: $_____

14. **What your assets will be
    worth when you retire**
    (multiply line 13 by a
    multiplier in Column B) $_____

15. **Additional savings needed**
    (subtract line 14 from line 12) $_____

Figure 12.1 20 Steps to Retirement Income Planning (Continued)

16. **Amount of savings needed each year** (multiply line 15 by a multiplier in Column C. If married, use the *lower* number of years left to save) .... $_____/yr.

17. **Estimated annual employer retirement plan contributions** (if any) . $_____/yr.

18. **Amount need to save per year** (subtract line 17 from line 16) .... $_____/yr.

	Husband	**Wife**

19. **Number of paychecks per year** _____ _____

20. **Amount needed to save per pay period** (divide line 18 by line 19) $_____ $_____

*If both spouses are employed, the total amount of retirement savings needed should be allocated between them according to a mutually agreeable arrangement.

Inflation-Adjusted Multipliers*

Number of Years in Retirement	Multiplier A	Number of Years Before Retirement	Multipliers B	C
10	9.8	5	1.10	.192
15	12.8	10	1.22	.091
20	16.4	15	1.34	.057
25	19.5	20	1.49	.041
30	22.4	25	1.64	.031
35	25.0	30	1.81	.025
40	27.4	35	2.00	.020
		40	2.21	.017

*Round off to the nearest five-year interval.

Most people have a gap between their desired retirement income and the amount provided by Social Security and employer benefits. According to 1990 Social Security Administration figures, Social Security provides an average of 36 percent of retirement income, and pensions provide 18 percent, for a combined total of only 54 percent. The remaining 46 percent comes from earnings, personal assets and other sources. The gap is largest for high earners because they get proportionately less from Social Security than low earners. Personal savings can often make the difference between being comfortable and barely getting by.

Some of your retirement capital could come from an anticipated inheritance or a capital gain on the sale of an asset such as real estate. Remember, though, a primary residence provides retirement capital only if its owner is able to sell it for more than it costs to buy another home. The rest of the money you need must be saved during your remaining working years.

Financial security in retirement has often been compared to a three-legged stool. Social Security represents one leg, employer-provided retirement plans, the second, and personal savings, the third. In order to keep the stool standing, all three leg are needed. Yet only 46 percent of American workers have pensions. Many workers, particularly part-timers, the self-employed and those who work for small businesses, simply don't have any employer-provided retirement benefits. Their stool is very wobbly, making personal savings imperative. Another model, shaped like an amoeba, was recently suggested in a financial industry publication to signify that retirement funding no longer has the stability it once had and will remain in flux as personal and economic conditions change.

Retirement Myths and Realities

Many people postpone saving for retirement because they mistakenly believe one or more of the following five myths:

1. My spouse will support me.

2. My children will support me.

3. Social Security will not be eliminated.

4. I won't need much to live on.

5. It's too early to start saving for retirement.

In years past, it was not unusual to see several generations living together under one roof, à la the Waltons (of the long-running television series). Future retirees, however, can no longer assume that they'll be cared for by either their families or the government. It's a demographic reality, for example, that women outlive men by an average of four years. This means there are five times as many widows as widowers among the population older than age 65. Regardless of who lives longer, pension and Social Security benefits are generally reduced when a spouse dies. Adult children often have career and family responsibilities of their own. They may not have the resources to financially support their aging parents or they might live thousands of miles away.

As far as Social Security goes, any politician voting for its elimination would probably vote himself or herself out of a job. But that's not the point. Social Security was always meant to be a base upon which to build and is, by itself, an insufficient source of income. For middle-income earners, Social Security will replace less than a third of preretirement earnings.

It's also a mistake to believe that you can live comfortably on less than half of your preretirement earnings. Many financial advisers recommend a figure of between 70 to 80 percent of preretirement income. With this assumption, a couple earning $40,000 prior to retirement would need $28,000 to $32,000 afterward to maintain their living standard.

Some reduction of income in retirement is possible because state and federal taxes are often reduced and work-related expenses, such as commuting and union dues, are eliminated. You also no longer have to pay Social Security taxes or set aside money as savings for retirement in accounts such as IRAs or 401(k) plans. Other expenses should also be less than before retirement. As your mortgage is paid off, housing costs will decrease. Life insurance policies may be paid up and disability insurance will cease.

Other expenses may increase once you retire. Health care costs and travel expenses are prime examples. Even though most retirees are covered by Medicare at age 65, supplemental health insurance is usually recommended unless employer-provided insurance continues into retirement. Routine medical and dental expenses may also increase because they are usually not covered by Medicare. If you plan to travel extensively or spend winters in a warmer climate, you'll also need additional funds.

Housing issues should also be considered years before retirement. You may wish to purchase a home in another area of the state or country now if you plan to relocate at retirement. Until then, the property can be rented or used as a second residence. Another major concern of retirees is the cost of health care. Find out now whether your employer's health insurance will extend into retirement and whether you or your employer is responsible for paying the premium. Some generous employers provide health insurance at no cost to retirees who meet required conditions, such as a specific length of service. Find out whether your employer is one of them and, if not, what your health insurance options are at retirement. Adequate coverage is especially important for early retirees age 55 through 64 because Medicare is unavailable.

It is important to remember that the concept of retirement planning is relatively new. Most people didn't live past working age several generations ago. Women, especially, need to plan ahead for retirement. About half of all women age 65 and older are widowed and 70 percent of all married women outlive their husbands. Those who put off learning how to take charge of their finances are usually the most disadvantaged.

In short, it's never too early to start planning and saving for retirement, particularly if you would like to retire before age 65. A logical place to start is with a list of your current assets and anticipated sources of retirement income. Next, calculate the amount you must save annually and per pay period to fill in the gap between what

you'll need and what you'll have. Then check to see
whether your employer offers a retirement savings plan
and make plans to start or increase your savings at work
or on your own.

Sources of Retirement Income

More than a dozen potential sources of retirement
income exist. Because several are employment-related,
not all are available to everyone. Sources of retirement
income include qualified employer retirement plans,
Social Security, annuities, continued employment or
free-lance work, IRAs, simplified employee pension
plans, salary reduction plans, Keogh accounts, dividends
and interest, rental income and capital gains on the sale
of assets.

Qualified employer retirement plans are those that
receive favorable treatment under specific sections of the
tax code. Participating employees do not have to report
as income the contributions made on their behalf by their
employer until benefits are actually distributed. Three
main categories of qualified retirement plans exist: **pension, profit-sharing** and **thrift plans**.

Pension plans are divided into **defined benefit** and
defined contribution plans. Defined benefit plans
offer participating employees a pension that is established in advance by a formula. The formula is usually
based on employees' salary or years of service or both.
Defined contribution plans are pensions where the payout to employees depends on investment results
achieved during years of accumulation.

It is important to become familiar with your pension plan when you're hired and not when you're about to retire. Workers with long records of service with one employer are generally rewarded with generous pensions. On average, workers with ten years of service can expect to receive 10 to 15 percent of their final salary. Those with 20 years of service can expect to receive 20 to 25 percent and career employees with 30 years of service can expect 30 to 35 percent of their final salary.

The second type of qualified retirement plan, **profit sharing**, ties employer contributions to the profitability, or lack thereof, of a company. An employer has the flexibility to vary contributions or to omit them completely. At retirement, employees can take their share in the form of cash or company stock. A related type of qualified plan, similar to profit sharing, is the **stock bonus plan**. With both plans, greater productivity by workers often results in a larger accumulation. The difference between the two is that stock bonus plan distributions are always made in the form of company stock rather than cash.

The third type of qualified retirement plan is the **thrift plan**. Employees are allowed to allowed to contribute after-tax dollars, generally 2 to 6 percent of their pay. Many employers also match employee contributions at a certain rate (e.g., 50 cents on the dollar). Interest accumulated in a thrift plan is tax deferred until withdrawal.

The second major source of post-employment income, for about 95 percent of the American workforce, is **Social Security**. In order to receive Social Security benefits, an individual must be fully insured, have reached at least age 62 and file an application. "Fully insured" means that the required quarters of coverage have been acquired, based on wages earned. Each year, the amount of earnings needed to earn a quarter of coverage is adjusted for inflation. Persons born after 1929 need 40 quarters of coverage to be fully insured.

Social Security has been called a pact between generations because it is financed on a pay-as-you-go basis. Revenues collected from today's workforce are used to pay current beneficiaries. The amount of Social Security that a person receives depends on personal (or a spouse's) lifetime earnings and the age at which benefit application is made. You can receive a Social Security check as early as age 62, provided you are fully insured, but your retirement benefit will be permanently reduced by $5/9$ of 1 percent for each month of retirement before age 65.

Starting in the year 2000, the age at which full benefits are payable will be increased in gradual steps until it reaches 67. This will affect people born in 1938 and later. Reduced benefits will still be payable at age 62 but the reduction will be larger than it is now.

If, on the other hand, you don't apply for benefits and you work past age 65, you receive a special credit. For each month that you delay receiving retirement benefits, beginning with the month you are 65 and ending with the month you are 70, you receive an extra amount in benefits when you do retire. The rate of this delayed retirement credit varies according to your year of birth. For people who reach age 65 in 1990 or later, the credit will be gradually increased until it reaches 8 percent in 2009.

Before the Social Security Administration unveiled a new computer program in 1988, it was often difficult for persons who were years away from retirement to get an accurate benefit estimate. Today, the agency can provide a personal earnings and benefit statement with estimates of future Social Security benefits at ages 62, 65 and 70. You'll also receive a summary of past earnings and estimates of survivor's and disability benefits. To receive a statement, contact your local Social Security office or call 1-800-772-1213.

It's a good idea to check your earnings record every three years to make sure that wages have been reported and posted correctly. You usually have only a limited period of time to correct any mistakes, such as transposed numbers or missing wages.

Annuities are a third source of retirement income. **Immediate annuities** start benefit payments shortly after purchase. They are bought with a lump sum, such as a pension distribution or an inheritance. **Deferred annuities** accumulate over time on a tax-deferred basis. They can be bought monthly, through periodic payments, or as a single-premium deferred annuity purchased with a lump-sum payment of at least $5,000. Funds accumulate tax deferred until retirement.

Fixed annuities guarantee your principal and a certain rate of interest for one to six years. Rates are then adjusted annually according to market rates during the life of the contract. **Variable annuities** combine mutual-fund-type investment options and tax-deferred returns. The investment return is tied to the performance of the underlying funds and your principal is not guaranteed.

Continued employment is another source of retirement income, whether in a new job, in your present position, as a consultant or as the owner of your own small business. About 3.5 million older Americans (12 percent) were in the labor force in 1990. It's important to plan your postretirement earnings carefully, however, because Social Security places a limit on how much you can earn before benefits are reduced. The earnings limit is adjusted annually for inflation. In 1994, if you're between the ages of 65 and 69, your benefit is reduced by $1 for every $3 earned above $11,160. For retirees younger than age 65, the 1994 reduction is $1 for every $2 earned over $8,040. After age 70, earnings limitations are no longer in effect.

Individual retirement accounts (IRAs) are a source of retirement income available to all wage earners younger than age 70½ and their nonemployed spouses. The maximum annual contribution allowed is the lesser of 100 percent of earned income or $2,000, plus an additional $250 for a nonemployed spouse. Earnings compound tax deferred until withdrawal at retirement, at which time they are taxed as ordinary income. IRA contributions can be made on the first business day of each year through April 15th of the following year. The earlier an account is funded, the longer earnings accumulate tax deferred. Over 30 years, assuming an average annual return of 10 percent, the difference between IRAs funded on January 1st and April 15th of the next year will exceed $42,000.

An IRA itself is not an investment. It is, rather, like an umbrella under which you can purchase a variety of savings and investment products, including, but not limited to, CDs, mutual funds, stocks, bonds, Ginnie Maes, real estate limited partnerships and American Eagle gold coins.

Simplified employee pension plans, or SEP/IRAs, as they are sometimes called, are a type of IRA provided by employers, especially small business and small professional corporations. The employer makes contributions to SEP/IRA accounts that are controlled by employees. By establishing an SEP plan, an employer does not have to contend with the cost and administrative complexity of a qualified plan.

The next category of retirement income, **salary reduction plans**, refers to savings plans that are established by employers: 401(k) plans for corporate employees, 403(b) plans for employees of schools, colleges and nonprofit organizations and Section 457 deferred compensation plans for county and municipal government workers. If you're self-employed, you're eligible to open a **Keogh account**. All have the advantage of allowing before-tax dollars to be set aside for retirement.

Other sources of retirement income include the interest or dividends earned on savings and investments, the positive cash flow generated by a rental property, a stream of income that you contracted for, such as a mortgage, and the capital gain on the sale of an asset.

How Much Do You Need To Save?

How much money a person must save for retirement depends on five primary factors:

1. How much retirement capital and employer benefits are already accumulated

2. The dollar amount of income needed

3. The number of years between now and retirement

4. The number of years a person expects to be retired (based on assumptions about life expectancy)

5. The growth rate on invested dollars

The first step in planning for financial independence in retirement is to look at where you stand financially today. The best way to do this is with a net worth statement (see Figure 3.2). Although you might be pleasantly surprised at your net worth, remember that not all your assets will be available as a source of retirement income. You will need your car(s) and personal property for day-to-day living, and all or part of your liquid assets for emergencies. Your home won't provide income unless you sell it and invest all or part of the proceeds.

The next step is to calculate your retirement income gap—the difference between what you need in retirement and what you can expect to receive from Social Security, employee benefit plans and current assets. Figure 12.1 assumes that your savings will earn 2 percent *after taxes and inflation,* both *before* and *after* you retire. If you don't select investments that provide this built-in inflation protection, you'll need to save more money.

The worksheet also assumes that you will spend your retirement income and assets during your expected lifetime and that of your spouse. If you want to leave an inheritance to your heirs, you must save more or exclude from your calculations the value of assets to be gifted to others.

Once you've done an initial calculation, try using the worksheet several more times with different assumptions for factors such as retirement age, desired income and life expectancy. This provides a reality test for your goals and a range of dollar amounts needed to save. If you are unsure of your future plans, err on the conservative side (e.g., fewer years to save and a longer life expectancy). It's better to have more money than you need than to have to restrict your living standard.

Remember, too, that retirement planning is an ongoing process. Your concerns at age 40 are likely to be quite different from those at age 60, 70 or 80. A comfortable retirement doesn't just happen. Your lifestyle as a senior citizen will almost certainly depend on how well you've planned for it.

13

Your House as a Bank— Leveraging Your Savings Through Real Estate

You have a number of ways to become wealthy. Among the most common are receiving a valuable item as a gift, inheriting a large sum of money, saving slowly but steadily in tax-deferred retirement plans, operating a successful business, winning a large lottery or contest prize and investing in successfully leveraged investment vehicles. Leverage is the use of someone else's money to magnify an investment's gain or loss. Well-chosen investments in real estate have generally produced a profit and have made many average wage earners wealthy over time. This remains true in the 1990s, even though real estate markets have cooled down.

A common example of leverage is the mortgage used to purchase your home. Let's assume that you purchased your home for $100,000. Ten years later, it's worth $200,000. A doubling of your money, right? Wrong! When you bought your home, you put, maybe, $20,000 down and took an $80,000 mortgage. Only a fifth of the original purchase price came from your own resources.

Today, your home is worth ten times more than your original investment. That's leverage!

Increasing home equity is a relatively painless method of saving money. Equity is the difference between your home's current value and its outstanding mortgages. Equity increases in two ways: by an increase in the value of a home (due to home improvements, inflation and local supply and demand factors) and as steady repayment of a mortgage over time reduces indebtedness. During the late 1970s and most of the 1980s, many Americans effortlessly sat back and watched the value of their homes rise. The largest portion of most Americans' net worth is their home equity.

You have several ways to convert your home into a "bank" and increase the value of your investment or the comfort of your surroundings or both. They include principal prepayment, well-timed trade-ups or trade-downs of property, the purchase of a second residence or investment property and home improvements that are popular with potential buyers. You may, for example, wish to purchase property in another area of the country now if you plan to relocate at retirement. Until then, the property can be rented out or used as a second residence. A second property will increase your net worth because real estate has historically been a profitable investment in most areas. Assuming a modest 3 percent average annual rate of growth, a $120,000 primary residence and a $70,000 second home will be worth $216,735 and $126,425, respectively, in 20 years, or more than $340,000 combined.

Starting Out or Trading Up:
Hints for Homebuyers

Buying a home is the largest purchase most people ever make. A homebuyer who doesn't shop around might spend a lot more money than is necessary. Comparison-shopping should take place at all stages of the home-buying process, including the hiring of professional advisers, the signing of a contract between buyer and seller and the selection of a mortgage. The difference between 8.5 percent and 9 percent interest on a 30-year, fixed, $100,000 mortgage, for example, is about $36 a month, or almost $13,000 over the life of the loan.

Before you can successfully purchase a home, you need information. Three to six months before you active-ly start shopping, begin to read the real estate section of local newspapers and the free real estate magazines available at brokers' offices. Note the location, size, fea-tures and, of course, price of listed homes. Determine whether prices appear to be rising or whether sellers are reducing their asking prices. A picture of a home with snow in front of it in a midsummer advertisement means the property has been on the market awhile.

Also, start reading the financial press, noting changes in median and average housing costs and the prime rate. These indicators track the two factors that will determine what you'll pay for a home: price and interest rates. Find out whether the Federal Reserve is expected to change the interest rate it charges member banks, which is reflected in the rate they, in turn, charge borrowers.

Let's assume that you're now actively searching for a new home. The first thing a buyer should do is line up an attorney and a home inspector. You'll need to use their services within days of signing a contract and it is helpful to establish a rapport in advance. When you start visiting homes for sale, keep a notebook to jot down your impressions and the key features of each. Plan to look at a minimum of 10 to 15 houses in your price range.

To determine how much home you can afford, most lenders follow two general rules. The first is that the total cost of a home (principal, interest, taxes and insurance) cannot exceed 28 percent of your gross monthly income. The other is that the total cost of a home plus other debt cannot exceed 36 percent of your gross monthly income. For example, if a couple earning $36,000 annually applies for a mortgage, their monthly mortgage payment would be limited to $840 ($3,000 a month times 28 percent). If the couple also had an existing $300-a-month car payment, their monthly mortgage payment would be limited to $780 ($3,000 a month times 36 percent equals $1,080; $1,080 minus $300).

Eventually, most buyers find a home they can afford that meets most, if not all, of their specifications. Now it is time to negotiate. The seller's anxiety level is an important consideration. Sellers may take less if they've had few offers, are buying another home, are divorcing, are settling an estate or must transfer to a new location quickly. Try to find out why a seller is moving, how long the seller's home has been on the market and whether the seller has had previous offers. You can negotiate from strength if you know something about the person you are dealing with.

You are now ready to sit down with a real estate agent and begin the negotiating process by submitting a contract. An important consideration is, of course, the home's price. As a general rule, sellers expect to receive less than their asking price and often pad it accordingly to get the amount of money they really want. Unless the real estate market is extremely active, you should present an offer below asking price. The exact amount of your offer will depend on how fair you think the asking price is and how fast local homes are selling. If your contract is not accepted, based on price alone, you can always resubmit a new contract and raise your offer. You usually cannot go back to a seller and lower your offering price once a contract is initiated.

Other aspects of a contract to buy a home deserve as much attention as the price. If you forget to put something in writing and your contract is accepted, it may be too late to add anything. Consider the following:

① **Items Included with the Sale**—If you would like to possess items such as the seller's refrigerator and crystal chandelier, say so in writing. The seller can then decide to include them in the offering price, increase the price accordingly, remove these items from the contract or sell them in a separate transaction. If you don't ask, you won't receive, so be specific to avoid misunderstandings.

② **Interest on the Deposit**—Be sure that the contract indicates that the buyer will receive the interest on the down payment. With 5 to 10 percent or more of the selling price placed in escrow for several months, the amount of interest earned can be substantial and can help pay the closing costs.

③ **Home Inspection Clauses**—Two out of every five homes for sale have at least one serious defect costing at least $500 to repair. A contingency clause should be written into the contract to allow the buyer to have one or more inspectors evaluate the property. This clause also allows the buyer to void the home purchase contract if inspectors find serious problems with the home.

Once a buyer has completed the contract, it is presented to the seller. If the seller accepts everything as is, the offer becomes binding on both parties, subject to any listed contingencies, such as a home inspection clause. If the seller wishes to negotiate, a counteroffer is made either with a new contract or with notations made on the original document. The buyer can then sign it, if it's acceptable, or reject it and make a second offer. Most agreements are reached after two or three rounds of offers and counteroffers.

Negotiate Like a Pro

Below are some additional tips to help you find the home of your dreams for the lowest price possible:

① During the time that you visit homes for sale and negotiate a contract, watch what you say within earshot of either a real estate agent or a homeseller. Everything you say can, and will, be used in the bargaining process. If you submit a contract with a figure lower than the asking price, don't let the seller's agent know that you are willing to pay more. Never confide your negotiating strategy. The agent is legally bound to persuade you to buy at full asking price and on terms that favor the seller.

② Don't respond to any suggestions or counteroffers unless they are presented in writing. If a seller or the seller's agent verbally tells you that your offer is too low, insist on a written counterproposal indicating the price (or other changes) that would make the offer acceptable.

③ Sellers are generally more willing to reduce prices from October through March, when fewer buyers look for homes. If the timing of your purchase does not depend on external factors like a job transfer, consider buying off-season. Also, consider waiting for a buyer's market, which is a period when there is more supply than demand and prices are flat or decreasing.

④ If a seller agrees to make repairs, based on negotiations following a home inspection report, insist that they be done by contractors you select. Otherwise, the work could be completed ineffectively with cheap labor or shoddy materials.

⑤ Under no circumstances should you submit a contract after seeing a home only once. Return for another look and again, if necessary. Remember, you don't really see a home on the first visit. Rather, you usually focus on several outstanding features (e.g., pretty wallpaper) and often have little or no recall, or an inaccurate impression, of the rest of the home. Returning to the home also provides an opportunity to engage the sellers in conversation.

⑥ Remember, most real estate agents work for and are paid by sellers. You may want to consider hiring a buyer's broker to represent your interests. You will be charged a flat fee, an hourly rate or a percentage of the sales price. A good buyer's broker should be a skilled negotiator and able to save an amount greater than or equal to the fee.

Negotiating to buy a home is the process of telling sellers at what price and on what terms you are interested in their property. Expect to haggle when you insist on the price and conditions you desire. Many buyers don't realize that they are allowed to bargain on key features of the deal and agents don't always tell them. Read real estate books and articles, consult knowledgeable friends, hire professional advisers where needed and ask questions. Doing your homework will help you buy a home with confidence and can save you thousands of dollars.

Negotiating the Mortgage Maze

Finding the right home is just the beginning of the home-buying process. The next step is to locate the right mortgage. A generation ago, the only two things home-buyers needed to know were the interest rate and the length of a loan. Today, things are not so simple. Homebuyers face a choice from among more than 100 varieties of mortgages and decisions about points, caps, application fees and lock-in periods. Most of these options evolved during the late 1970s and early 1980s when inflation reached double digits and lenders began to adjust mortgage interest rates to changing economic conditions.

It's best not to wait until a contract is signed to begin the search for a mortgage because the time period in which to obtain a loan commitment is relatively short. Methods of obtaining information about mortgages include calling lenders directly, asking a real estate agent or attorney for suggestions and subscribing for several weeks to a mortgage-rate reporting service. As you make plans to finance a new home, here are six tips to consider:

① **Put More Money Down**—If you have ample savings or expect to receive a substantial profit from the sale of a current home, you can reduce your mortgage substantially by making a 20 to 30 percent down payment. The difference between 8.5 percent, 30-year $80,000 and $100,000 loans is $154 a month, or more than $55,000 over the life of the loan.

② **Compare Points**—Don't ignore the impact of points when comparing mortgage loans. A point is a prepayment of interest at (or before) the closing and equals 1 percent of the loan amount. On a $100,000 mortgage, for example, three points costs $3,000. The length of time you remain in a home should determine whether you choose a lower mortgage rate with more points (recommended if you stay more than five years) or a higher mortgage rate with fewer or no points. The annual percentage rate (APR) of a mortgage measures its total interest cost, including points, and can help you make comparisons among fixed-rate loans.

③ **Consider an ARM**—If you're stretching to qualify for a mortgage, a one-year adjustable rate mortgage
(ARM) will usually buy the most home for the lowest
initial interest rate and monthly payment. The interest
rate on ARMs is adjusted periodically according to a
specified index to reflect changes in market conditions.
As the index rises or falls, mortgage rates change
accordingly: every year for one-year ARMs and every
three years for three-year ARMs. A major advantage of
ARMs is that their initial rate is often up to 2.5 percent
less than that of a fixed-rate loan, thereby enabling borrowers to qualify for a larger mortgage. The difference
in interest rates occurs because the risk of rising interest rates is partly ¿   med by the borrower. If interest
rates decline or hold steady, payments will not increase.
If interest rates rise, however, payments will also
increase.

Fortunately, for some protection against rising interest
rates, most ARMs have caps, or limits on rate changes.
Most rate changes are capped at two percentage points
annually and a maximum of 5 or 6 percent over the life
of the loan. The downside is that in cases of large rate
increases negative amoritization can occur. This means
that the amount of mortgage debt is increasing, although
payments are being made. When shopping for an ARM,
ask about the maximum annual and lifetime interest rate
increases and limits for the amount of negative amoritization. Then consult a mortgage payment table to find
the corresponding monthly payment and consider
whether you could afford the loan under a worst-case
scenario.

④ **Lock In a Rate**—If you fear that interest rates will rise, look for a lender that will lock in a mortgage interest rate and guarantee it in writing for the period of time between application and closing, which is usually at least 45 days and preferably 60.

⑤ **Shorten the Loan**—Growing equity mortgages (GEMs), biweekly mortgages and 15-year mortgages build equity much faster than other types of mortgages and save thousands of dollars of interest. Also known as rapid payoff loans, **GEMs** are fixed-rate, fixed-term mortgages. Generally, beginning in the loan's second year, monthly payments are increased by an agreed-upon percentage, with the extra amount earmarked to reduce principal. GEMs are typically repaid in 12 to 15 years.

Biweekly mortgages have fixed rates. Instead of making one mortgage payment every month for 30 years, you make half of a monthly payment every two weeks. With 26 payment periods per year, you make the equivalent of 13 monthly mortgage payments and the loan is repaid in about 20 years because the extra month's payment is applied to principal.

Fifteen-year mortgages feature a fixed rate and monthly payments. Because the loan is repaid in 15 years instead of 30, borrowers pay much less interest over the life of the loan. Generally, lenders also charge a slightly lower interest rate on 15-year mortgages than on 30-year mortgages because their money is at risk for half the time. For instance, a 15-year, 8.5 percent, $100,000 mortgage will cost $177,300 to repay, less than two-thirds of the cost of a comparable 30-year loan. The trade-off is that the shorter maturity requires monthly payments that are about 20 percent greater than on a 30-year, fixed-rate mortgage. For example, the above-mentioned mortgage will cost $985 per month for principal and interest while a 9 percent, 30-year, $100,000 mortgage will cost $805, or $180 a month less.

⑥ **Prepay Principal**—Prepayment of principal on a 30-year mortgage will reduce the amount of interest charged and retire the loan years sooner than scheduled. With as little as an extra $25 a month, homeowners can save thousands of dollars over time. The reason is that paying off a loan balance sooner than scheduled prevents a lender from collecting interest on the prepaid amount. Principal prepayment has its greatest impact when a mortgage is new because the principal portion of monthly mortgage payments is small.

Mortgage prepayment is a more flexible arrangement than either biweekly or 15-year mortgages because you're not locked into mandatory twice-monthly payments or a higher fixed dollar amount. During the holiday season, or when you're short on cash, you can pay just the minimum monthly payment required, with no additional prepayment. If you receive a raise or bonus, you can prepay more. Most mortgages don't have prepayment penalties. In fact, mortgage coupons often provide a space marked "additional principal paid." A homeowner interested in principal prepayment can either obtain a loan amortization chart to determine the exact amount of principal contained in upcoming mortgage payments or remit any extra amount, such as $25 or $50, to the lender.

Enhance Your Largest Asset:
Home Improvements That Pay

Many people buy homes knowing that they'll sell within three to five years. Perhaps it's their starter home or they plan to have a larger family or their employer transfers them frequently. If you're in such a situation, think carefully about the payback of various home improvements. A general rule is that you cannot expect to sell a home for more than 20 percent above the neighborhood average. This is because the value of a home is largely determined by the value of the homes surrounding it. If you buy an $80,000 home in a $100,000 neighborhood, you probably shouldn't spend more than $40,000 to improve it. A five-bedroom house on a block of starter homes is simply out of place.

Among the most profitable home improvements, according to recent surveys of appraisers, are carpeting, paint and wallpaper, kitchen and bathroom renovations and a fireplace or deck additions. Other enhancements that generally return at least 50 percent of their cost are landscaping, a central air conditioner, exterior painting and a garage or room addition. Energy conservation features that decrease ongoing utility costs are another wise investment. Hot tubs and pools, on the other hand, can actually detract from the value of a home. Some buyers view the maintenance, extra electric bills and potential for lawsuits negatively and will by-pass a home for this reason. At the very most, expect to recover no more than 35 percent of the amount spent. If your only concern is creating a home where you can live happily for a long time, by all means improve it in whatever way you choose. If you are concerned about a not-too-distant resale, make only improvements that buyers want and are willing to pay for.

Remember, a home is considered a capital asset. Like any other investment, capital gains taxes must be paid when it is sold for a profit. One way to reduce this future tax burden is to save all records pertaining to capital improvements as soon as a home is purchased (see Chapter 11). Use Figure 13.1 to get started. Capital improvement records should be placed in a file separate from annual tax records and saved for as long as you own your home, plus at least three years.

Figure 13.1 Capital Improvement Diary

Improvement	Location	Cost	Date Completed
Aluminum siding	Home exterior	$3,500	9/88
Wall-to-wall carpeting	Living/dining room	$2,000	4/91
New furnace	Basement	$5,000	3/93

Capital improvements are not the same as repair or maintenance activities (e.g., painting walls or fixing broken glass). A capital improvement must add to a home's value, prolong its life or adapt it to a new use. Repairs just maintain a home in its current condition.

Each time you sell a home, you must complete IRS form #2119, "Sale or Exchange of Principal Residence." It asks you questions such as how much you paid for your home and how much you sold it for. You should always retain this form because you will need to refer back to it for subsequent home purchases and sales. One home sale affects the cost basis of the next and you must track how much profit you're deferring.

Selling Your Home: How To Increase Your Bottom Line

Unless a home is refinanced or sold, its owner's equity is merely a paper profit. When the time comes to sell, however, a homeowner is in a position to receive one of the largest sums of money ever accumulated in a lifetime. A little time and money spent early in the selling process can result in a profit of thousands of extra dollars. Below are five tips to consider:

① **Compare Prices**—Before you list your home with a real estate broker (or sell it yourself), ask one or more real estate firms to give you a complimentary market analysis. An agent will visit your home and estimate its value by comparing it with recently sold homes of similar size and condition in your area. The service is free and there is usually no obligation. You could also hire a professional appraiser, who will charge about $500 to thoroughly evaluate your home.

② **Increase Curb Appeal**—Curb appeal is the appearance of your home to prospective buyers who drive by. To encourage them to explore further, remove all clutter (e.g., old cars, bikes, tree limbs). Keep the lawn mowed and hedges trimmed. Sweep the walks and replace dead trees. Look at your home with a critical eye, as a potential buyer would. Stand across the street and see how it looks from a distance. If you need to spend some money to spruce up your property, save your receipts. Any repairs made within 90 days of its sale can reduce your capital gain. Some examples of exterior fix-up repairs include touching up shutters, window sashes and trim; replacing roof shingles; landscaping; and installing vinyl or aluminum siding.

③ **Cleanliness Counts**—A clean, attractive home is easier to sell than one that needs work. Some suggestions for sprucing up a home include removing or cleaning badly soiled carpeting; removing soiled wallpaper and repainting walls with off-white paint; repairing leaky faucets; repairing nicks in paneling, wooden doors and molding; mending broken tiles in the bathroom; repairing hardware and hinges on doors; and neatly arranging decorative items such as throw pillows and plants. Arrange furniture to give a feeling of spaciousness and organize furnishings and closets so they appear tidy. Paint, carpeting and wallpaper should be kept to neutral tones so that buyers won't have to contend with colors that don't match their furnishings. One of the easiest and most valuable home improvements is an interior face-lift. This means sprucing up the inside of your home with new paint, wallpaper, carpet and linoleum. A clean, bright home tells potential buyers that you care that your home is in good condition.

④ **Beware Prospective Buyers**—Try to have as few people as possible around when your home is shown. Children should be kept occupied and pets tied up outside. Unless you're selling the home yourself, let your real estate agent do the talking. The less contact sellers have with prospective buyers, the less chance they have of saying or doing something that can jeopardize a sale.

⑤ **Evaluate Offers Carefully**—Before you sign any sales contracts, know your bottom line—the amount of money you'll net after subtracting a lawyer's fee, fix-up costs, possible state realty transfer taxes and a real estate broker's commission, if applicable. Factors in addition to the price should also be considered, such as the amount of a buyer's deposit and resources and home sale contingency clauses, which make a buyer's purchase of your home contingent upon the sale of his or hers.

Remember, when prospective buyers tour your home, they have probably already calculated the approximate monthly mortgage cost. If they see loud colors and worn or broken fixtures, they'll add the cost of things that must be redone or repaired to the mortgage cost and weigh your home along with others they've seen. Perceived problems can translate into a lower offer or a foregone sale.

A home is the most important purchase most people ever make and one of the wisest investments, too. While stock and bond values can fluctuate greatly, housing prices generally hold their own. In addition, owners can live in their home while they pay for it, can defer taxes on capital gains and can make a purchase with as little as 5 or 10 percent of the purchase price.

Leverage and the time value of money are a powerful combination. A homeowner who makes a $30,000 down payment on a $150,000 home earns 15 percent ($4,500 ÷ $30,000) if the home appreciates 3 percent, to $154,500 in one year. After 20 years, if it appreciates by the same amount, the total return is a healthy 400 percent! The disadvantages of real estate as an investment are that it takes time to sell and may entail legal or sales expenses. Regional markets also tend to become soft from time to time, thereby reducing homeowners' appreciation.

Disadvantages aside, the increase in value of a home over time can provide funds for retirement, a child's college education or other financial goals. Negotiating the best deal at purchase or sale can save thousands of dollars over time and well-chosen home improvements and principal prepayment can increase both home equity and net worth.

14

You Can't Take It with You—
Estate-Planning Basics

If you were killed in an automobile accident, would your possessions be distributed as you desire? Would there be a legal guardian named for your children and one or more persons you trust designated to settle the financial affairs of your estate? Do you have a will to ensure that your property is distributed according to your wishes, with minimum delay and expense? Has your will been reviewed and, if necessary, updated lately?

If you answered yes to one or more of the above questions, you've already done some estate planning. Estate plans are the provisions people make to use or give away property while they're alive or after their death. It is the orderly transfer of assets to designated entities such as family members or charitable organizations. A will is a necessary component, along with trusts, life insurance, joint and individual ownership of property and the beneficiary designations on pensions and individual retirement accounts (IRAs).

Contrary to popular myth, you don't need the portfolio of a Donald Trump or Bill Gates to have an estate plan.

All you need is some property, in which case you will probably require a simple estate plan, perhaps only a will. Estate planning should be done by virtually all adults and any others who possess significant assets in their own name. You certainly don't want to save money on a shoestring all these years, only to have the IRS or some attorneys take the lion's share.

The advantages of estate planning are numerous and include the ability to designate specific assets for certain beneficiaries, a voice in the distribution of property you've worked a lifetime to acquire and potentially larger bequests to survivors or charity through a reduction of taxes and legal expenses. Lifetime gifting as part of a well-designed estate plan also provides an opportunity to teach beneficiaries financial planning skills, such as management of a stock portfolio. It may be a better learning experience for your heirs and a wiser use of your money to make one or more small, supervised bequests during your lifetime than to leave a substantial sum after your death.

Despite its numerous advantages, estate planning is done by only a small fraction of Americans. It is estimated that seven out of ten people die without a will, leaving their assets to be distributed by state courts and court-appointed administrators. Why is it that people who spend a lifetime working, accumulating an estate and caring for a family and loved ones leave the distribution of their property to the state?

One reason is procrastination. Many people, especially young couples and singles, feel that they are too young or have plenty of time to think about estate planning. Buying a home, raising a family and even planning for retirement come first in the minds of many people. Unfortunately, young people also die from accidents, crime, cancer, even heart attacks. An estate plan, particularly a will, provides for the unexpected while allowing flexibility for the future. Plans can be revised as household assets or personal circumstances (e.g., death, divorce) change.

Another reason for the lack of estate planning is superstition. Many people regard the discussion of heirs and executors as some sort of jinx. Other people simply dislike lawyers and legal documents and avoid them at all cost. Still others feel that they don't have enough money to worry about or that all of their property would ultimately go to their spouse anyway.

While many people truly don't have much money in bank accounts or investments, they probably have life insurance policies, retirement savings plans or a home. Chances are they have an estate worth $100,000 or more. Young families have something even more valuable than property—minor children. In the rare but possible case that both parents simultaneously die intestate (without a will), a state court must appoint a guardian to act on behalf of the children. The selection could be someone who wouldn't have been the parents' first choice and will involve added expenses, such as annual accountings of funds and the posting of bond.

As for the belief that your spouse will inherit all of your assets, this is generally *not* the case when someone dies without a will. In just a handful of states, a spouse receives the entire amount of a deceased partner's estate. In all other states, a spouse is entitled to only a percentage (generally one-third to one-half) of assets, and children or other close relatives (e.g., parents of a deceased spouse in a childless couple) receive the rest. The state could award funds to minor children, who can't spend anything without a court-appointed guardian, while a spouse is left with a severely reduced standard of living.

In the case of stepfamilies, lack of a guardian named in a will can cause a costly and emotional custody clash between a child's surviving biological parent and his or her stepparent. If the biological parent is estranged from the child, the stepparent, although possibly a more loving and suitable choice for guardian, could be passed over because stepparents legally have no responsibility to support someone else's children. By naming a stepparent guardian in a will, you provide the stepparent with at least some basis for contesting custody, although no guarantee of success.

Simultaneous deaths cause another set of problems, especially for childless couples without a will. If one spouse outlives the other by even a fraction of a second, all of the couple's assets can be inherited by the parents of the second spouse to die. According to the laws of intestacy in many states, the second spouse to die is considered to have inherited all of his or her spouse's assets de facto during the time interval between their deaths. The assets, in turn, become the property of the second-deceased's parents, even though the parents of the first to die might have a greater need for the money and share the same sense of loss and grief.

When There's a Will, There's a Way

A will states how you want your property divided and who you want to handle your financial and personal affairs after your death. Very few documents you sign are as important. With a will, you can

- determine to whom, how and when your assets will be distributed;
- name an executor who will manage your estate (if you die without a will, the state decides who will settle your affairs);
- create trusts for your spouse, children or others, thus providing income for beneficiaries;
- reduce and sometimes eliminate estate taxes;
- make gifts to charitable organizations (a charitable organization can't inherit assets from a person who dies intestate);
- reduce estate administration costs (e.g., bonding and accounting fees);
- name a guardian for minor children in the event that both biological parents die;
- teach dependents or beneficiaries money management skills; and
- avoid confusion and conflict among survivors.

Among the items likely to be included in a wall are the name and address of the person making the will (this person is called the testator), the date that the will was signed, a revocation of all prior wills, a list of beneficiaries and the amount of assets given to each, specifications about the timing of bequests to heirs, the appointment of a guardian for minors and an executor to supervise the distribution of assets, and the signature, name and address of at least two witnesses. In the case of married individuals, a common disaster clause is often added to dictate how property is to be distributed if both spouses die simultaneously.

If you don't have a will, you won't have a voice in how your assets are distributed when you die. The state may do just what you would have wanted or it may not. Not having a will leaves a lot to chance. You may not be able to make a gift to someone or some organization, such as your favorite charity, hospital or university. If you die without a will, the court will appoint an administrator for your estate. This person will most likely, but not necessarily, be a family member and must be bonded until the estate is settled.

Wills should be written—or at the very least, reviewed—by an attorney to avoid possible complications or challenges. The fee for having a will prepared should not be a major roadblock. Charges vary from about $100—$150 for a simple will to several thousand dollars for a complete estate-planning package (the fee usually depends on the amount of time required to prepare the documents). Whatever the cost, relatively few dollars spent now can save your family heartache and many thousands of dollars when you die. The fee for bonding an administrator alone ($3 to $10 per $1,000 of estate value) is considerably more than the cost of preparing a will.

If you don't yet have a will, make an appointment with your attorney as soon as possible. If you don't have an attorney, ask a friend to recommend one or contact the local bar association for a referral. Because you will pay for an attorney's time, go to your meeting prepared. You may be able to lower the final cost by doing some homework first. Bring with you the names and addresses of your proposed executor and guardian and persons designated to serve as alternates, a complete list of the names, ages and addresses of family members, information about previous marriages, a net worth statement, the names of those you wish to inherit your assets, and a list of items you wish each beneficiary to receive. If you have a business or professional practice, specify how it should be transferred or disposed of.

Once your will is completed, keep the original document in a safe place, such as an attorney's vault or your executor's safe-deposit box. Let one or more persons know where the will is but not necessarily the contents. Some individuals do an excellent job of hiding their wills—such an excellent job, in fact, that the wills are never discovered. If no will is located, a person is presumed to have died intestate.

If you already have a will, review it periodically and make necessary changes when state and federal estate tax laws change or if you change marital status, adopt or give birth to a child, move from one state to another, buy a home, accumulate additional capital or loan large sums to relatives (unless you have a provision in your will to forgive a debt, your executor is obligated to collect all unpaid loans). If you change any portion of your will, you must write a new will or update the present one with an amendment called a codicil. Never cross out sentences or remove pages. If you have named a guardian, a trustee or an executor who has since died, appoint another individual, and perhaps an alternate, to fulfill these responsibilities.

The Unified Credit and Estate Taxes

Picture an extremely wealthy individual dispensing generous gifts to friends and loved ones minutes before death. The survivors subsequently become instant millionaires and the government ends up with nothing. Possible? Not on your life! The federal Unified Gift and Estate Tax ensures that Uncle Sam receives his fair share and encompasses all asset transfers made from one party to another, regardless of timing. Whether you give away assets while you're young and healthy, on your deathbed or in a will, the government requires that they be included in gift and estate tax calculations.

The federal estate tax is a tax based on an individual's net worth at death. Like income tax rates, federal estate tax rates are progressive in nature. This means that, the more your estate is worth, the higher the rate of tax it will pay (during the time that a deceased's affairs are being settled, his or her estate becomes a tax-paying entity). For estates valued at more than $500,000, tax rates of between 37 and 55 percent are charged. Estates valued at more than 3 million dollars face the 55 percent levy.

While the word *estate* can be defined broadly as "everything you own," the estate tax people at the IRS are actually interested in a deceased's *gross estate for federal tax purposes,* which includes the following assets:

- All property owned outright in the deceased's name alone (e.g., cars, savings and investments, real estate, personal property)
- All property owned jointly with others with a right of survivorship. This means that if a joint tenant dies, his or her share automatically passes to the surviving joint tenant(s). If the property is owned jointly with a spouse, half of its value is added to the deceased's gross estate, regardless of which party actually provided the funds to purchase the property. If the property is owned jointly with someone else, its full value is included in the estate of the first to die unless the surviving co-owner can document his or her contribution.
- The decedent's share in property held as a tenant in common with others. Tenancy in common is a form of ownership where owners can sell their interest without consulting the other owners and decide who inherits their shares following death.
- All life insurance policies owned by the decedent, paid to the decedent's estate or transferred to others within three years of the decedent's death
- The value of all gifts made by the decedent within three years of death (the IRS assumes that we can anticipate our demise with plenty of advance notice)
- Transfers where the decedent retained income, control or the right to revoke or amend a gift.

By now, you're probably wondering just how much of the fruits of your labor will be confiscated by Uncle Sam in the form of federal estate taxes when you die. Fortunately, for most people, the answer is very little, if any. Three perfectly legal and generous tax breaks, when properly used, protect the average American's estate from paying any federal estate tax whatsoever.

The first estate tax break, available to all individuals, is the *unified credit*. This credit allows you to give away during your lifetime and leave in your will up to $600,000 of assets free of gift or estate taxes. The credit is cumulative and the amount available decreases as it is used over time. Since 1987, the unified credit has been holding at $192,800, which effectively shelters $600,000 (called the *exemption equivalent*) of estate value from taxes.

It's important to note that gift and estate tax rates became one and the same following passage of the Economic Recovery Tax Act of 1981. The unified credit was increased from an exemption equivalent of $275,000 in 1983 to its current $600,000 amount. Multimillion-dollar estates, far in excess of the unified credit, are still subject to high estate taxes, which is why wealthy individuals are urged to seek professional guidance in planning their affairs with trusts, annual gifting and other tax-reduction strategies.

For middle America, the unified credit is usually sufficient to eliminate any estate tax, although this may not be the case forever because the exemption equivalent is not indexed for inflation. If the entire credit is not used, however, it is lost (no such thing as an estate tax refund exists). For example, on a $500,000 estate, the estate tax of $155,800 would be more than offset by the $192,800 unified credit but the estate would not get any money back.

The second estate tax break, which is also available to all individuals, is the *annual gift tax exclusion*. This exclusion shelters from gift tax gifts made during your lifetime, thereby preserving the $600,000 exemption equivalent for use at a later date. Individuals can gift up to $10,000 per year in cash or property to any number of individuals without having to file a gift tax return and use their unified credit. If a husband and wife jointly make a gift to the same individual, the annual exclusion is doubled to $20,000.

Of all the taxes average Americans could pay, gift taxes are probably the least understood because we're not in the habit of making five-figure gifts to others (when was the last time you gave someone $10,000?). Without such a tax, however, large estates held by wealthy individuals could go virtually untaxed if assets were transferred quickly to others in anticipation of death. With an annual gift tax exclusion of $10,000 per person per year, it would take the wealthy many years to dispose of their assets (the government is betting on this) without using any of their $600,000 exemption equivalent. The key concept to remember is that, as long as annual gifts to individuals are less than the $10,000 exclusion amount, the full $600,000 exemption equivalent remains available to offset future estate taxes.

The third estate tax break, available only to married couples, is the *marital deduction*. When the marital deduction is used, gifts from one spouse to the other are completely exempt from either federal gift tax or estate tax, regardless of the dollar amount. Property can be transferred to a spouse as a lifetime gift, in a will, by state laws of intestacy, through joint ownership of property or by the beneficiary designations on legal contracts such as life insurance policies.

While the marital deduction sounds like an ideal way for couples to reduce estate taxes, it can backfire in more affluent households and result in a greater overall estate tax (and fewer assets for heirs) following the death of the surviving spouse than would have been the case if household assets were more evenly divided. In households with estates in excess of $600,000, professional estate-planning advice is strongly recommended to compute the precise marital deduction necessary for the estate of the first spouse to die to pay no estate tax after using the unified credit and other available estate tax deductions. No more marital deduction should be claimed than is necessary and the unified credit available to the estate of the first to die should not be wasted.

A popular strategy to reduce the estate tax of married couples with more than $600,000 of taxable assets is a credit shelter trust. It provides for placing $600,000 (the amount of the current unified credit exemption equivalent) in a nonmarital trust and gifting the balance of the estate—outright or in trust—to the other spouse. This has the effect of splitting an estate in two pieces and keeping the amount in the nonmarital trust out of the estate of the second spouse to die, where it would be heavily taxed. It also accomplishes the goal of earmarking assets for children or charitable organizations.

It is possible, and often very effective, to combine the use of the unified credit, annual gift tax exclusion and marital deduction. As an example, consider Mr. Smith, who is married with two grown children, who are also married and trying to purchase their first homes. Mr. Smith's estate is currently valued at $440,000 and his wife's, at $340,000. The Smiths divide their estate by gifting each *couple* a one-time-only $40,000 ($20,000 to each spouse from both Mr. Smith and his wife) free of gift tax for home down payments and closing costs. This reduces the Smiths' estates to $400,000 (Mr. Smith) and $300,000 (Mrs. Smith). Mr. Smith then divides his estate by leaving $300,000 to his wife and $100,000 ($50,000 each) to his children.

The $300,000 is exempted from tax by the unlimited marital deduction and the $100,000 is sheltered by the unified credit. Assuming Mr. Smith dies first, when Mrs. Smith dies, she can leave whatever remains of the $300,000 she inherits, plus the $300,000 of assets currently in her own name, to the two children and it will be sheltered by her unified credit. The result is that no tax is paid on either the lifetime gifts or the estate of either spouse who dies. Naturally, this plan must to be reviewed and revised as the value of the Smiths' assets changes.

Yours, Mine and Ours: Joint Ownership of Property

It is a common misconception that joint ownership of property is an effective substitute for a will. It isn't. In fact, several serious problems can occur, costing thousands of dollars of needless estate taxes and administrative costs. One major problem is that, by owning all of their property jointly, a married couple ensures that it will be automatically transferred to the estate of the second spouse to die. As noted previously, estates exceeding the $600,000 exemption equivalent are taxed at rates beginning at 37 percent. With other forms of property ownership and a well-drawn will, married couples can shelter $1.2 million, or twice the exemption equivalent, from federal estate taxes. If these numbers sound too rich for your blood, think again. Over a working lifetime, a middle-income couple earning, say, $30,000 to $40,000 each year could amass a sizeable estate.

A second problem occurs when there's a conflict between joint ownership with a right of survivorship and other property transfer arrangements, such as a will. The result is an unintended disinheritance and often a legal challenge by angry would-be beneficiaries, costing thousands of dollars. Generally, the right of survivorship of jointly owned property is presumed to supersede any other property transfer arrangement. It's important to review will and trust documents carefully to make sure they are not in conflict with property ownership arrangements.

One common situation in which unintentional disinheritances can occur is when elderly persons place bank or brokerage accounts in joint tenancy with only one child (generally the one who lives the closest) for the convenience of handling routine financial affairs, such as depositing Social Security checks and paying bills. This child, alone, will inherit all jointly held assets and can deprive siblings of an equal share of the parent's estate if so inclined.

Another common situation involves remarried persons

who jointly title assets with their second spouse, despite the fact that their will provides for the transfer of this property to children from their first marriage. As noted previously, a joint ownership provision usually takes precedence over a will when the two conflict. The children can receive nothing because their stepparent automatically inherits the assets and is under no obligation to share them.

When used properly, however, joint ownership has its advantages. It's convenient (one account instead of two), provides an automatic transfer upon death and serves as tangible and symbolic proof of the joint owners' trust and togetherness. Because the surviving joint owner is automatically the beneficiary of an asset, some people feel that a will is not needed. Remember, though, that estate planning is more than just distributing property. To name an executor and a guardian and engage in certain tax-reduction strategies, you must have a will.

Common Estate-Planning Errors

① **Failure To Draft a Will**—Without a will, a deceased's assets are distributed according to state intestacy statutes. In most states, spouses, children and parents are designated as beneficiaries, although the division of assets varies from state to state. Without a will, it may be impossible to make bequests to unmarried cohabitants, close friends, siblings or charitable organizations. The administration of an estate is also likely to be more expensive, resulting in smaller distributions to heirs.

② **Failure To Revise a Will**—After a will is drawn, it shouldn't be tucked away and forgotten. Instead, it should be reviewed and revised periodically. Situations in which a will may need updating include marriage, separation or divorce; the birth of a child or grandchild; a move to another state; the death of a named beneficiary or executor; substantial increases or declines in net worth; changes in state or federal estate tax laws; and changes in your distribution of assets.

③ **Poor Recordkeeping**—Without some inkling of the location of key documents, like a will and life insurance policies, an executor and survivors could spend months, even years, looking for them. Make it easy for everyone concerned with a detailed list that includes the names and addresses of financial advisers; the amount, policy numbers and location of insurance policies; the account numbers and location of banks and brokerage firms where you have accounts; the location of important personal papers; and an inventory of your safe-deposit box, including the location of the key.

④ **"I Love You" Wills**—This term is often used to describe wills where everything is left to a surviving spouse. As noted previously, this could result in higher estate taxes upon the death of the second spouse. To avoid this situation, both spouses should plan to take full advantage of their estate's unified credit. Trusts should be considered as a tax-reduction strategy for those with gross estates exceeding $600,000.

⑤ **Failure To Anticipate Growth of an Estate**—It's important to think in terms of the future when planning your estate. It may not exceed $600,000 now but it could in the future. Estate value should be monitored periodically and plans revised as asset values increase.

⑥ **Need for Power and Control**—Some people resist transferring assets to others to reduce estate taxes due to the powerful emotions they have regarding money. They view a lifetime gift as a loss of control over assets and therefore by-pass the potential benefits of the annual gift tax exclusion or marital deduction. The ultimate beneficiary of their need for control is often Uncle Sam. Failure to take advantage of gift and estate tax deductions can result in higher taxes.

⑦ **Improper Life Insurance**—While life insurance policy proceeds are distributed outside of a decedent's probate estate (those assets administered by an executor before distribution to heirs), they are included in the gross estate for federal tax purposes. Persons who own large amounts of life insurance they no longer need (e.g., parents whose children are grown) should reevaluate their coverage.

⑧ **Lack of Liquidity**—Persons who own substantial but illiquid assets (e.g., a farm or business) can leave their heirs in the position of owing estate taxes and having little or no readily available cash to pay the bill. Life insurance can be purchased to provide the estate needed liquidity or, in the case of business interests, a buy-sell agreement among the shareholders or partners can be drafted. This avoids the problem of having to cash out of the illiquid asset—to pay taxes—at a fire-sale price.

⑨ **Poor Business Asset Planning**—Many business owners lack plans for the operation of their business upon their death. Business succession planning guarantees an orderly transfer of what, for many business owners, is their largest single asset.

⑩ **Poor Choice of Executor**—Performing the duties of an executor requires both time and organizational skill. Never choose as an executor a person who appears unwilling or who is extremely busy or incompetent in financial affairs. Delays and mistakes can cost your beneficiaries dearly.

Estate planning, like financial planning, is not just for the rich and famous. The plans you make today can affect your family's lifestyle for decades to come. Many people also prefer to limit the influence of government on their lives. Preparing an estate plan, especially a will, is one sure way to keep the government out of your personal affairs.

15

Beyond the Cookie Jar—
Women's Changing
Financial Needs

Forty years ago, it was not uncommon to hear women's earnings referred to as pin money. This implied, often incorrectly, that a woman's income was not considered essential to her financial well-being or that of her family. Another popularly held belief was that women kept their money in a sugar bowl or cookie jar because it was not considered important or permanent enough to earn interest in a bank account.

If the practice of stashing money in a cookie jar was ever as widespread as depicted, it is certainly not the norm today. Career woman or homemaker, single or married, many women today make important financial decisions.

Changing family roles are a major reason for women's increased interest in financial planning. Large numbers of women entered the labor force in the 1970s and 1980s and began earning their own incomes. By 1991, more than half (57 percent) of women ages 16 and older were employed, including 58 percent of mothers with children younger than age six. In 1960, only one in five mothers of preschoolers worked outside the home.

During the 1970s and early 1980s, inflation began to escalate. The Consumer Price Index (CPI) rose more than 50 percent between 1978 and 1983 while incomes often barely kept pace with price changes. Consumers, who between 1940 and 1970 enjoyed three decades of progress in per capita income, saw their real income go up at only miniscule annual rates in the 1970s. Economic need, as well as career goals, sent increasing numbers of women into the labor force. Many of these women are better educated than previous generations and their salaries make a large impact on the lifestyle of their households.

Is Demography Destiny?

Demographic trends are a second reason that women need to be concerned about money. Many women will live alone for some portion of their lives. Among the major reasons are the high incidence of divorce and out-of-wedlock births in the United States and women's longer average life expectancy compared to men. In 1991, the median incomes of different types of households were as follows:

- Married couples, both spouses employed $48,169
- Married couples, husband only employed $30,075
- Male-headed families $28,351
- Female-headed families $16,692

The trend toward more women heading single-parent families is projected to continue. Almost one in eight families was headed by a single parent in 1991, double the proportion in 1970. Five times as many single parents are women, mothers who are widowed, divorced, separated or never married. Approximately half of all American marriages end in divorce.

Also, during the past two decades, the 65-and-older population increased twice as fast as the rest of the country's population. In 1990, older men were almost twice as likely to be married as older women, with 77 percent of men older than age 65 married, compared to only 42 percent of similar-aged women. Not surprisingly, older women have a higher poverty rate than older men. According to the American Association of Retired Persons, the median income of older persons in 1990 was $14,183 for males and $8,044 for females.

Women's Earnings

A third argument for sound financial planning by women is the wage gap, the differential between average men's and women's salaries. Women need to manage money more carefully than men because they usually have less money to manage. In 1991, the Bureau of Labor Statistics of the U.S. Department of Labor reported that women earned 74 cents for every dollar earned by men, up from 59 cents in 1977. In recent years, most of the narrowing of the wage gap has occurred because men's wages have fallen, not because women make more money.

The Good News

Fortunately, several important federal laws and changes in the financial services industry have benefited women.

Federal Credit Legislation

Married women who make an effort to establish a credit history have gained access to credit in their own name. The Equal Credit Opportunity Act made it unlawful for creditors to discriminate against applicants on the basis of gender or marital status in determining their creditworthiness. The act prohibits discriminatory practices such as refusing credit to qualified married women who apply for a separate loan or charge account, refusing to consider alimony or child support as income, asking about applicants' childbearing plans, requiring a spouse or another cosigner for unsecured loans by creditworthy borrowers and terminating or revising the terms of a credit transaction based on changes in marital status.

Unfortunately, some women today still find themselves disenfranchised by the world of credit upon divorce or widowhood. They simply have no credit histories and are invisible to both lenders and credit-reporting agencies. The Equal Credit Opportunity Act only makes it easier for married women to establish a credit history. It is up to all women, married or single, to create their own identity. Among the steps recommended for those who have never used credit are opening a savings or checking account in their own name, acquiring charge cards in their own name (having credit often gives a person access to more credit) and establishing a preapproved credit line at a bank. Married women should advise lenders that they want shared accounts reported in their own name as well as their husband's (e.g., Joan Smith and John Smith) and check with at least one major credit bureau to make sure that their record is on file.

Federal Estate Tax Legislation

Before the early 1980s, some widows found themselves paying federal estate taxes on property they helped to maintain and accumulate. This was especially true for the wives of farmers and small-business owners, who often worked alongside their husbands and contributed significant time and labor to the family business. Things have changed. The Economic Recovery Tax Act, which became effective in 1982, provides for unlimited tax-free transfers between spouses and a $192,800 unified estate and gift tax credit (see Chapter 14), which protects $600,000 of transfers that aren't sheltered by the marital deduction. In most cases, widows in all but the most affluent households are no longer required to pay federal estate taxes on property, such as a primary residence, which often increases in value to far more than its original purchase price. During the past decade, some state legislatures also eliminated, phased out or reduced state inheritance taxes or marital transfers.

Increased Purchase of Insurance and Investments by Women

As large numbers of women became employed, banks, brokerage firms and insurance companies saw a market developing and began to target their products and services to female clients. Female wage earners require life and disability insurance coverage comparable to that of their male counterparts and, as their incomes grow, also have more disposable income to manage.

Pension Reform

The Retirement Equity Act of 1984 contained a number of helpful provisions benefiting women. In the past, many women received few, if any, pension benefits from plans with formulas weighted to reward high income and long years of service. Today, there is no loss of previous service credit for breaks in work of up to five years, nor does maternity leave of up to one year count as a break. Recognizing that some women enter the workforce early and interrupt their careers to raise families, the law also lowered from 22 to 18 the age at which pension plans begin counting service for pension vesting purposes.

Another 1984 pension law change entitles the spouse of an employee who qualifies for an annuity but dies before retirement to a survivor annuity. Most importantly, the Retirement Equity Act requires the written consent of a spouse before joint and survivor pension benefits can be waived. When a joint and survivor annuity option is selected, the monthly payment is generally reduced but the employer continues payments after the death of either the husband or the wife. Formerly, many women, who usually outlive their husbands, didn't learn that their husbands had them elected out of a pension until after the funeral.

The 1984 law also authorized, but does not require, courts to treat a spouse's pension as a joint marital asset that can be divided as part of a divorce settlement. This provision is especially valuable for women who are full-time homemakers for a majority of their married years.

The Tax Reform Act of 1986 also contained some key pension reform provisions. Private pension plans had to reduce the number of years a person must work to be fully vested from ten to five or use a 7-year graded formula instead of a 15-year one. Social Security integration could no longer offset pensions by more than 50 percent, entitling lower paid workers to at least some pension benefit. Previously, many lower paid workers (especially women) never received a pension benefit because their Social Security, which was greater, offset all of it.

The Bad News

Despite the improvements in women's finances, some significant problems remain:

Financial Illiteracy

Women are the beneficiaries of most life insurance policies and represent more than half of all individual shareholders. And yet, for the most part, the wealth owned by women is not actively managed. Women, as a whole, are more conservative than men in their investment choices, preferring safety to high returns. A 1992 study also found that women save only half of what men do, on average.

Due to inertia, fear or lack of knowledge, some women invest to keep their capital intact without realizing that they are losing purchasing power. For example, a taxable passbook savings account yielding 3.5 percent today returns only 2.52 percent after taxes to persons in the 28 percent marginal tax bracket and even less after state and local taxes are deducted. With inflation averaging 3 to 4 percent during the past few years, the owner of a passbook account is losing money!

Fortunately, these attitudes toward money appear to be changing. A widely quoted study conducted in 1992 by Oppenheimer Management found that 88 percent of more than 1,000 women interviewed felt confident that they could invest a $10,000 windfall. Of more than 1,000 men interviewed, 93 percent felt that their wives could handle their finances alone if they had to. More than 95 percent of the men and women surveyed said financial decision making was a joint effort, with more than half of the married women paying the bills. Almost half (43 percent) of the women surveyed said they enjoyed thinking and talking about investing and a full 82 percent believed that they would someday be solely responsible for their financial well-being. Several recent publications have also suggested that women often make better investors than men because they admit what they don't know, ask questions, seek assistance and follow the advice they are given rather than attempt to outsmart the financial markets.

Inadequate Retirement Income

Many older women, particularly those who took time out from paid employment to raise their families, have lower incomes in retirement than their male peers. Social Security and most pension plans use benefit formulas based on an earner's salary and years of service. Persons with lower earnings and gaps in service are, therefore, at a disadvantage.

Social Security assumes a 35-year work history and drops the lowest five years of earnings for a worker with 40 years of employment. For workers with less than 35 years of Social-Security-covered earnings, however, each year without earnings counts as zero in the average, resulting in a lower benefit. Lower paid, employed wives whose husbands also pay Social Security tax may receive no benefit from their own contributions. The spouse of a retired worker is entitled to the greater of one-half of a retired worker's full benefit at age 65 (37.5 percent if benefits are elected at age 62) or the benefit determined by his or her own earnings record. Few women earn incomes greater than or equal to the maximum wage base ($60,600 in 1994) to receive maximum benefits.

Compare the pensions of two soon-to-retire workers whose benefit formula is: number of years of covered service times 1.4 percent of the average of the three highest years' salary. Jane has participated in the pension plan 15 years with a $20,000 high-three salary. Sally has participated in the pension plan 30 years with a $50,000 high-three salary. Their annual pension benefits are $4,200 and $21,000, respectively.

As greater numbers of women earn higher salaries, work full time and take shorter breaks for child-rearing, gaps in the retirement incomes of men and women should decrease. Currently, however, more than two-thirds of the elderly poor are women. Women can no longer assume that they will be protected. Instead, they should plan for the distinct possibility of widowhood. Those who have put off learning how to care for themselves are usually the most disadvantaged.

Displaced Homemakers

In 1975, the phrase *displaced homemaker* was coined by activist Tish Sommers to describe women, formerly full-time homemakers, forced to reenter the workforce because of a spouse's death, desertion, disability or divorce. Most lack recent job experience, training and education and nearly 75 percent are age 55 or older. The older a displaced homemaker, the more likely she is to be unemployed and to have a lower educational level. The Displaced Homemakers Network, a coalition of displaced homemaker organizations nationwide, has called this phenomenon "the dark side of the women's movement" because of the misperception that the much-publicized progress of some women is progress for all women.

Displaced homemakers are often too young for Social Security or may be ineligible because of divorce from the family wage earner. A spouse must have been married to a worker for at least ten years to qualify for benefits. If the spouse does qualify and is experiencing financial difficulty, he or she may need to apply for benefits early (at age 62 rather than age 65), thereby receiving a reduced amount.

Without their husbands, displaced homemakers may also be cut off from health insurance and pension plan protection. If their children are older than age 18, the homemakers are often ineligible for public assistance. The 1986 Consolidated Omnibus Budget Reconciliation Act (COBRA) allows unemployed persons to retain group health coverage for up to 18 months by paying both the employer and the employee premiums plus a 2 percent administrative charge. The mandated coverage period is extended to 36 months for those who depended on a spouse for coverage if loss of coverage occurs because of the death, divorce or legal separation of the covered employee. Coverage applies, however, only to policy beneficiaries who are covered by a group health plan at the time a qualifying event (e.g., death, divorce) occurs. The cost of insurance is also prohibitive for many lower income households.

The White Knight Syndrome

Among some women and teen-aged girls today, there still flourishes an attitude that they will find a white knight to protect them. This attitude breeds dependency and vulnerability. Women who feel they don't have to earn an income or become knowledgeable about personal finance often never do. As a result, their repertoire of financial planning experiences and knowledge remains quite limited.

For most neophyte investors, men and women alike, the world of finance is like a foreign country with its own language and culture. To the uninitiated, words like *T-bills, single-premium deferred annuities* and *limited partnerships* are an alien, intimidating vocabulary. Women characteristically are more apt to ask for help than men and are currently educating themselves about personal finance in record numbers. As a person's knowledge and experience increase, so will his or her future financial security.

10 Tips for Financial Self-Sufficiency

Listed below are ten money management tips that can increase the financial self-sufficiency of both women and men:

① **Plan Ahead**—Define your financial goals completely, using both cost and deadline (e.g., a new car costing $12,000 in 1996), and develop and implement a plan of action to achieve them. Use the worksheet in Figure 2.2 as a guide for future planning.

② **Save Money**—Save 5 to 10 percent (or more) of each paycheck as soon as you receive it. Try using one or more of the saving methods listed in Chapter 5.

③ **Defer Taxes**—Take maximum advantage of employer retirement savings plans such as SEP/IRAs, 403(b) plans or 401(k)s. Both the money that is contributed to these plans and the earnings on contributed funds grow tax deferred until withdrawal.

④ **Don't Overspend**—Maintain a good credit rating in your own name and don't overload yourself with debt. Consumer debt, excluding a home mortgage, should not exceed 20 percent of take-home pay. Use the worksheet in Figure 9.1 to evaluate your current debt load.

⑤ **Plan Your Taxes**—Know your current marginal tax rate so you can project how much of your income is earmarked for Uncle Sam.

⑥ **Plan Some More**—Take advantage of tax-favored investments such as an IRA, rental real estate or your own home.

⑦ **Divorce Carefully**—Recognize the tax consequences of different divorce settlements and study the alternatives before you make a binding agreement.

⑧ **Plan Your Estate**—Make a will so that assets can be distributed as you wish rather than as state law decrees. Review and revise the will as estate tax laws and personal circumstances change.

⑨ **Keep Learning**—Educate yourself about personal finance by attending seminars, reading the financial press and seeking information from financial professionals. Research has shown that knowledge of investments is a significant variable in an individual's willingness to take investment risks. The more investment information acquired, the higher the risk inclination.

⑩ **Sharpen Your Skills**—Maintain and develop your career skills and ability to earn an income. This is one of the best investments you can ever make and a good insurance policy for the future.

Figure 15.1 provides a summary of financial do's and don'ts for women.

During the past quarter-century, fundamental changes have occured in the lives of American women. Some have called women's increased employment one of the most profound phenomena of the 20th century. Some women, however, continue to handle money as did women of generations past. They avoid making decisions, choose low-yield investment products and depend entirely on the support and decision making of others. This is a mistake. A comfortable retirement doesn't just happen. A woman's lifestyle as a senior citizen will almost certainly depend on how well she's planned for it during her preretirement years.

The old adage "a woman's work is never done" seems more true today than ever before as employment has become the norm. Busy schedules and increased responsibilities, combined with all the factors noted above, demonstrate the need for conscientious financial planning. Through the possession of wealth, women have become a major economic force. Today, it's not an option for women to be financially informed—it's a necessity.

Figure 15.1 Women's Financial Do's and Don'ts

Do's	Don'ts
Remember, love and marriage are not reasons for abandoning your individual financial identity.	Never allow yourself to drift into a pattern of joint ownership without knowledge of the implications.
Maintain and develop job-related skills and your ability to earn a living.	Don't allow your investment in higher education or job-related skills to become out of date.
Educate yourself about personal financial planning so that you can be an equal partner in family financial decisions.	Don't depend on the financial knowledge of others, allowing them to make decisions that affect your life.
Communicate openly about finances with your spouse, especially in stepfamilies where child support or alimony is an issue.	Never allow the household financial obligations and conflicts of a prior marriage to become a problem in the next.
Consider carefully the income tax consequences of various divorce settlements.	Don't request taxable alimony when money provided by an ex-spouse is really needed for child support.

Figure 15.1   Women's Financial Do's and Don'ts (Continued)

Do's	Don'ts
Learn the details of employer health and benefit plans so there are no surprises.	Don't wait until your 50s or 60s to begin planning and saving for retirement.
Make sure you maintain a credit rating in your own name.	Don't let your individual credit rating lapse by using a spouse's account.
Save a part of each paycheck by paying yourself first.	Never wait to see how much money is left at the end of the month.

16

He Works, She Works—
Financial Planning for
Two-Paycheck Families

What do ATM machines, all-night supermarkets, child-care centers, fast-food restaurants, microwave ovens and stores that deliver appliances on weekends have in common? They're all in demand by two-paycheck families, the dominant family model among workers. Few events have more dramatically affected family organization, roles and financial decision making than the large increase in the number of two-paycheck households. This change as well as reduced savings and increased use of credit are the three major ways families coped with rising prices during the late 1970s and the 1980s.

If you look at recent advertisements, you'll notice that retailers have geared their pitches toward the two-paycheck family. The television commercial stereotype of the housewife who cleans, scrubs dirty collars or cooks on screen has been replaced, at least in prime time, by women who earn their own money and drive their own cars and by couples who complain that they are too busy or too tired to undertake domestic chores. The service sector of the American economy continues to grow rapidly as two-paycheck families eagerly pay others to perform tasks they no longer have time for.

Government policymakers have also noticed two-paycheck families now that such families have become the rule rather than the exception. They observed second paychecks helping unemployed persons cope with job loss and some families still living reasonably well. With the passage of the 1986 tax reform law, unemployment benefits became fully taxable. In 1982, the child-care credit was increased according to a sliding scale based on household income. The credit provides at least some relief to two-income families with a dependent child or parent.

Two-paycheck clout influences consumer spending patterns and also manifests itself in more subtle ways. To many, jobs are less critical when a family brings in two paychecks. Many two-paycheck couples also consider both partners' income and career plans when making job-related decisions and may turn down promotions or transfers if the change does not benefit both.

The two-paycheck lifestyle is a necessary or preferred one for many couples and it is doubtful we could ever return en masse to the 1950s notion of the family in which Dad works full time and Mom stays home. People are simply not in the habit of adjusting their financial expectations downward. In addition to the financial advantages of two incomes, some couples report a closeness that develops when they understand the pressures of each other's work and participate in shared decision making.

The Power and Value of Money

For many people, discussion of financial matters is difficult. Traditionally, it has been considered in bad taste and an invasion of privacy to ask others how much they earn, how much one of their possessions cost or even when they will repay a small loan. Before marriage, few couples discuss their attitudes about money for fear of misinterpretation ("Is he/she marrying me for my money?"). When the subject of money *is* discussed, it is usually in the abstract (e.g., the high cost of living) rather than specific (e.g., how each person handles his or her finances).

Money is usually defined as a medium of exchange but it is much more. It is one of the strongest motivators of human behavior. Money colors the way people feel about themselves, their loved ones and their jobs and is often used to express emotions like anger, love and guilt. Money also implies power and this power of the purse can be significant. Many marital power struggles involve resentments that grow from feelings of dominance or dependence created by money.

In "traditional" marriages of years past, with the husband as sole wage earner, he, more often than not, had the last word on how the family income was spent. But now, with more wives working, the traditional balance of power has shifted. For a two-paycheck couple new to the arrangement, this change can be difficult. "I work now so I'd like to make some decisions" is a common desire of recently employed wives. Their husbands, on the other hand, may feel threatened. One study found that the balance of power within a family is altered according to the percentage of total family income a wife earns. The larger her contribution, the greater her power in family decisions.

No matter what each spouse earns, it is important to remember that financial squabbles are usually a symptom, not a cause, of marital distress. It is, therefore, vital that a couple address the underlying behavior. Emotional attitudes toward money rarely develop overnight. Instead, they are influenced over time by family upbringing, education, personality traits and life experiences. Attempting to combine two sets of values, as well as two incomes and two sets of assets and debts, is never easy. Small wonder that many financial counselors have added a pyschological dimension to their work by exploring their clients' deep-seated emotions about money.

Joint or Separate Accounts?

Whether you started married life under the assumption that you would both work or you are changing from a single-income to a double-income couple, you must decide what to do with the second income. "That's easy," you say. "It will help pay the bills." Or "More money means more enjoyment for the whole family." In day-to-day living, however, it often isn't that simple. First, you have the mechanical tasks of bill paying and recordkeeping. With both partners spending more time away from home, you must develop a system that works.

A second issue concerns a shift in the balance of

power caused by a second wage earner. Below are some questions with which couples often need to grapple:

- Should each spouse have money that is not account-able to the other—money that is his or hers, to do with as that person pleases?
- How should bills be paid? Divided down the middle, each spouse taking responsibility for separate items (e.g., the mortgage)? The husband responsible for all the basics, and the wife, all the frills? Jointly?
- Should the spouse who earns more have more say in financial decisions?
- Will both spouses live on one income and save the other for a special purpose, such as the down payment on a home?

How you choose to divide your earnings will be reflected in the way your savings and checking accounts are held: jointly, where both husband and wife have access to the money, or separately, where only one spouse's name is listed on the account. Both types of accounts have advantages and disadvantages. With a joint account, couples often enjoy a greater sense of shar-ing, of it being "our" money. On the minus side, couples can have problems when one signer predeceases or voluntarily leaves the other. In the case of a divorce or separation, the first spouse to reach the bank with a with-drawal slip could legally take all of the couple's funds.

Having a separate account, especially for women, can help establish a credit rating. When applying for credit, a person can show that he or she has assets to draw upon, if needed. Another advantage is that the money is clearly in the name of one person. Upon the death of either spouse, the survivor would have his or her own money to pay expenses until the estate is settled. And should a marriage end, each spouse could not spend the other's money. Separate accounts are also helpful when one spouse has a unique financial obligation like alimony or parental support. On the negative side, some couples report that keeping their money in separate accounts makes them feel like roommates rather than spouses.

Once the issue of joint and separate accounts is settled, couples still must face the question of how to divide their joint earnings. Listed below are three different ways that two-paycheck couples can handle their money:

① **Equal-share couples** deposit an equal amount (e.g., $500) of their respective salaries into joint savings or checking accounts to pay for basic expenses and shared financial goals. The remainder of their paychecks can be used as each spouse sees fit. Advantages of this system are that each spouse helps pay for household expenses and also has some money to call his or her own. Problems can arise, however, when one spouse earns more than the other. The lower earner might resent the higher earner's greater discretionary income. A recent report from the Bureau of Labor Statistics found that married women who work provide about a third of their family's income, on average.

② **Proportional-share couples** contribute a percentage of their salaries to cover household expenses and savings goals, based on each spouse's contribution to total household income (e.g., he contributes 65 percent; she, 35 percent). The remainder is theirs to do with as they please. On the plus side, both spouses contribute to household expenses based on their ability to pay. A possible problem, again, is resentment if the numbers aren't fully agreed upon or adjusted for changes in salaries and expenses.

③ **Pooler couples** combine all of their income to use for both household and personal expenses. An advantage of this method is that the work of each spouse is valued equally, regardless of the amount earned. A part-time worker or a spouse who earns much less than the other is not penalized in his or her discretionary purchasing power when a difference in earnings exists. A disadvantage is that either spouse may feel obligated to discuss all purchases with the other, leading to spending squabbles or resentment. This is why many experts suggest that both spouses keep an independent allowance. This helps maintain sense of sharing while allowing each spouse to make purchases that are not accountable to the other.

Many married couples start out with one banking arrangement and gradually gravitate toward another. A young couple with few assets might start out by putting all of their limited funds into one pot. However, as each spouse earns more money, the couple might establish separate accounts as well, eventually ending up with three pots. On the other hand, remarried couples who begin their financial life together with unequal assets and responsibilities (e.g., child support) and scars from a prior relationship might feel more secure starting out with totally separate accounts. They may eventually merge all or part of their funds when they feel more sure of the relationship. The longer a couple is married, the more likely they are to move toward a one-pot or a three-pot system.

Earning and Spending Together

A great uneasiness exists among consumers today. Many feel that their standard of living is eroding and that their aspirations are being thwarted. Two-income households have median earnings about 60 percent greater than those of single-earner families. Nevertheless, they still must plan carefully to reach future financial goals. You and your spouse can get started by answering the following questions:

- Are you both satisfied with your current jobs?
- If not, how would you rather earn a living and what type of training is needed?
- What are your prospects for salary increases and promotions?
- How many years of gainful employment do you both have left?
- Are retirement and insurance benefits provided by your employers?
- Do you expect any changes in your personal lives to alter your financial situation?

Next, look at your spending habits. A second paycheck can provide a false sense of security and make it easy to qualify for his and hers credit cards, with the potential for a larger debt load. Married couples also must analyze the way they use and abuse money. For example, people sometimes buy gifts they really can't afford to make up for personal time they are not willing or able to share.

Some people are compulsive in their spending behavior while others can control this aspect of their lives. Those in the compulsive category may wish to initiate some safeguards: avoid shopping centers, carry little money and leave credit cards at home. Another way you can control spending is to track your expenses for a few weeks (see Chapter 4). Also, note your mood and whom you were with, if anyone, when you made purchases. After a few weeks, take a red pen and circle those purchases that were impulsive, unnecessary or induced by feelings such as guilt or anger. Once you are aware of your spending habits, you can begin to make changes.

Some couples control their spending by agreeing that neither will spend more than a given amount without first discussing the purchase with the other. Often, they find that, upon further reflection, the urge to buy a particular item is gone. It may also be helpful to discuss how money was handled in your respective homes. Was credit seen as shameful or as a way to increase your standard of living? Who had the power position in your home regarding money? Were financial decisions made in a cooperative manner or through argument, the silent treatment or other disruptive ways? Many times, when two spouses come from different socioeconomic or ethnic backgrounds, communication about money can prevent arguments and increase understanding.

Money Management Strategies for
Dual Earners

The financial planning strategies of two-paycheck families are often noticeably different than those of their single-earner peers. One reason is that there are two wage earners to protect through insurance against loss of life or disability. Another is that two wage earners give a family more financial stability. Should one spouse lose his or her job, the salary of the other keeps them going.

It is important, when reviewing life and health insurance plans, to consider the financial contributions of both spouses. Although most two-paycheck families need some life insurance, they usually need less than a single-earner family because the surviving spouse has an income.

Another area of concern is health insurance, particularly when both spouses are enrolled in group plans and benefits overlap. If policies are provided at no or low cost, it is probably best to keep them both because some plans allow for coordination of benefits. This means that, after you submit your claim to your own employer's health insurance plan, you can submit the claim again, with documentation of how much the first plan paid, to your spouse's employer plan for reimbursement of all or part of the balance. If, on the other hand, either or both of you must contribute to an employer health plan with duplicating coverage, you'll save money by dropping the less attractive plan. Another strategy to avoid duplicate coverage is to choose other types of fringe benefits in a cafeteria-style benefit plan if either employer offers one.

These plans allow workers to design their own benefit package by selecting different types of tax-free options funded with employer dollars.

Two-paycheck families also get treated differently tax-wise. Despite recent tax law changes that decreased the number of tax brackets, many dual-income couples filing jointly continue to pay more income tax than two single persons earning the same income and filing separately. This is because the first dollar of a married worker's salary is taxed not on its own but at the point in the tax brackets where his or her spouse's income ended.

Why does this happen? Tax laws are usually written in piecemeal fashion, often with unforeseen results. When the federal income tax system first began in 1913, citizens filed individually, based on their own income. In 1948, Congress reformed the system and established separate tax rates for married and single persons. However, this reform penalized single persons and, when Congress passed another reform to cut single-earner taxes in 1971, the "marriage tax" was inadvertently started.

How much does the marriage tax cost you each year? You pay the difference between the taxes you would owe as two singles and a married couple filing jointly. It is estimated that 52 percent of all U.S. couples will be affected by the penalty in 1994 and will pay an average of $1,244 more than if they were single and living together. The penalty tends to be greater when earnings increase and is greatest when both spouses earn approximately the same amount. Because of the marriage tax, two-paycheck couples often face the problem of tax underwithholding. This happens when neither of their employers withholds enough tax each pay period to cover the couple's joint tax liability. Underwithholding is especially a problem when one or both spouses have more than one employer withholding tax payments. To avoid this problem, claim fewer withholding allowances or request that a specific amount of extra money be withheld from each paycheck.

Figure 16.1 provides a summary of financial do's and don'ts for married couples.

Figure 16.1   Financial Do's and Don'ts for Married Couples

Do's	Don'ts
Share your feelings about money with your spouse. Find out each other's dreams, fears, risk tolerance levels and preferences for saving, investing and using credit.	Don't let past notions about money management dictate how you make financial decisions. The way your parents handled money may not be the best method for you.
Learn to compromise by adjusting some of your financial habits. Remember, there is no right or wrong way to handle money—only the way that works for you.	Try not to be judgmental about your spouse's method of handling money. Calling your spouse a tightwad or a big spender will only make him or her angry and defensive.
Set financial goals together. You are more likely to succeed if both spouses are committed to work toward a common purpose.	Never assume that you already know what's important to your spouse and that he or she automatically knows what you want.

Figure 16.1   Financial Do's and Don'ts for Married Couple (Continued)

Do's	**Don'ts**
Maintain at least a small separate bank account as well as some form of credit in each spouse's own name. Check credit ratings frequently.	Don't feel that individual accounts are unromantic. If you and your spouse have very different ways of handling money, they can help prevent money squabbles.
Examine each spouse's health insurance and fringe benefit package carefully to determine whether it might be advantageous to merge or drop coverage.	Don't pay for duplicate group health insurance and fringe benefits. Drop the less attractive plan and save the money you would have spent on premiums.
Turn squabbles about money into opportunities to discuss values and goals and to develop strategies for dealing with future financial issues.	Never use money as a weapon by retaliating with a purchase when your spouse seems distant or buys something you consider to be unnecessary.
Maintain a designated amount of individual mad money so you don't have to answer to your spouse for every penny spent.	Try not to feel guilty if you spend a relatively small amount of money without first consulting with your spouse.

Figure 16.1   Financial Do's and Don'ts for Married Couples (Continued)

Do's	Don'ts
Make time to discuss financial matters regularly, especially when only one spouse is responsible for recordkeeping; and the other needs to be kept abreast of where the money goes.	Don't feel that both spouses must be involved in every routine decision. In many households, bill paying is a chore that can be more effectively performed by one person.

Double-income couples are here to stay because working women, once the exception, are now the rule. As a result, questions such as "Who pays the mortgage?" and "What's 'your' money and what's 'my' money?" will be asked in more and more households.

Financial planning for two-paycheck families is, in many ways, more complex than for others. Two sets of income must be tracked and meshed on tax returns. And each spouse may have fringe benefits and require life and disability insurance in proportion to his or her contribution to household income. Nevertheless, the basic principles of financial planning hold true for working couples. A thorough discussion of future financial goals, coupled with an understanding of household net worth and cash flow, can go a long way toward helping working couples get ahead in the years to come.

17

Help—I Need Somebody! How To Choose Financial Advisers

If you needed legal advice, would you visit a law library and prepare your own case? How about a car repair? Would you open the hood and start tinkering? Would you extract your own tooth or prescribe your own medicine? Of course not! While these questions seem ridiculous on the surface, they emphasize an important point. Most people seek specialized professionals to do the things they are not trained for, are incapable of doing or lack interest in. This is especially true when our health is involved. Should our money be any different? Think about it. Your job requires skills, knowledge and abilities acquired through years of study, hard work and experience. Developing and implementing a financial plan also requires time, knowledge and ability. Just because you've received a paycheck over the years doesn't mean you are a skilled money manager.

Perhaps the most important reason for seeking professional advice is time—or, rather, the lack of it. Financial planners can save you both time and money. If you had to investigate all of today's available investment options and monitor their performance, you'd have little time for anything else. Financial planners, on the other hand, earn their living dealing with economic issues and may have dozens of specialized sources of information that individual consumers and public libraries are not privy to. Financial planners can generally provide more information more quickly than you could gather it yourself.

Hiring a professional financial adviser won't get you off the hook, however. You're still ultimately responsible for your financial goals and the actions taken to achieve them. You will, however, have one less thing to think about on a day-to-day basis and can concentrate on developing your own area of expertise and on your family. Many busy financial professionals, in fact, hire their own advisers so they can concentrate exclusively on their clients.

Financial planning was one of the fastest growing services of the 1980s. Financial planners help clients define and achieve their financial goals. Areas of personal finance included in a comprehensive financial plan include self-assessment and goal setting, insurance, savings and investments, taxes, retirement planning and estate planning. Financial plans can vary from hand-written notes on a legal pad to 50-page to 200-page computer-generated documents.

Presently, little regulation of the financial planning industry exists. Therefore, the term *financial planner* is used freely by persons in a variety of finance-related businesses. In addition to thousands of small financial planning firms nationwide, insurance companies, stock brokerage firms, banks, accountants and some attorneys offer financial planning services.

Many people wonder whether and when they need a financial planner. Generally, households with rising incomes that lack the time and expertise to manage their financial affairs benefit the most. A financial planner may be able to cut their taxes or help them make pre-retirement plans. In situations like divorce and the death of a spouse, a planner can provide information to help clients make important time-specific decisions.

Listed in Figure 17.1 are some common reasons given for seeking the assistance of a financial planner. Review the situations and check those that apply to you and your family. The more items you check, the more likely you'll benefit from a financial planner's services.

Choosing a Financial Planner

"We've just inherited $25,000 and we need help deciding where to invest it. So far, everyone we talked to who called himself or herself a financial planner just wanted to sell us something. Is there anyone out there who can give us objective advice?"

The above complaint is sometimes heard among consumers of financial services. Because many people could serve your financial planning needs, finding the right adviser is a challenge. A financial planner will help you make important decisions about the future; therefore, you have the right to expect a high standard of performance. Persons who discuss investment products before conducting an extensive client interview are using financial planning as a marketing ploy and should be avoided. Likewise, stay away from persons promising large prof-

Figure 17.1   Reasons for Seeking a Financial Planner

- ❏ Annual household income exceeding $50,000
- ❏ Federal income tax exceeding $5,000 annually
- ❏ Household assets exceeding $100,000 (excluding a home)
- ❏ Receipt of a windfall from an inheritance, gambling or a lump-sum pension distribution
- ❏ Gross federal estate exceeding $600,000
- ❏ Double-digit interest-rate certificates of deposit (CDs) or bonds, worth more than $10,000, coming due at a time when double-digit rates are no longer available
- ❏ Desire to change spending habits and increase personal savings
- ❏ Need to save money for a child's college education
- ❏ Need to save money for retirement
- ❏ Lack the time and expertise to make major investment decisions
- ❏ Need help understanding insurance policies and employee benefit programs
- ❏ Significant lifestyle change such as marriage, promotion, divorce, widowhood, birth of a child or purchase of a home

its or huge tax write-offs, and avoid telephone investment solicitations.

How do you determine whether a financial planner is a qualified professional? One way is to ask about the approach he or she would take to your plan, which should follow the seven-step process outlined below or some variation of it:

Step 1—Obtain pertinent financial data (e.g., net worth) and other information from client.

Step 2—Discuss client's future financial goals and risk tolerance.

Step 3—Agree on repositioning of current assets, if any.

Step 4—Review spending patterns and develop a spending plan.

Step 5—Furnish a written financial plan to client.

Step 6—Help client implement the plan.

Step 7—Follow up periodically to review and revise the financial plan.

Perhaps the most misunderstood aspect of choosing a financial planner is the virtual alphabet soup of professional designations following their names. Some of them have special significance while others do not. The most misused acronym is IRA (registered investment adviser). According to the Investment Advisers Act of 1940, persons who sell securities or provide investment advice are required to register with the Securities and Exchange Commission (SEC) as a registered investment adviser by completing a form called the ADV and paying a $150 fee. No educational or experiential qualifications are required, however, nor does registration imply any government certification or endorsement of a particular financial planner.

Yet, some financial planners use RIA after their name as if it were a professional designation because it sounds official (registered nurses and registered dieticians have to earn their credentials!) and impressive. Beware: Any professional purporting to be a financial planner who uses only the letters RIA should be questioned about his or her other qualifications. The designations that do have academic importance and indicate advanced study are as follows:

- *CFP*—certified financial planner. Persons who complete a program of study approved by the Certified Financial Planner Board of Standards in Denver, Colorado, earn the CFP designation. The CFP is the most widely held financial planning designation, with almost 28,000 CFP licensees as of early 1994.
- *ChFC*—chartered financial consultant. Persons who complete a series of ten courses through the American College in Bryn Mawr, Pennsylvania, earn the ChFC. Many are insurance courses, with additional courses in topics such as investments and taxation. Most graduates also hold the chartered life underwriter (*CLU*) designation, which indicates proficiency in the area of insurance. There are approximately 15,000 ChFCs nationwide.
- *CPA*—certified public accountant. Persons who have gone through a series of tax-related training and examination earn this credential.
- *JD*—juris doctor (attorney). Look for an attorney who

has completed a course of legal study in issues related to personal finance and who has been admitted to practice in a particular state or states.

- *MSFS*—Master of Science in Financial Services. Persons who complete advanced coursework at accredited colleges and universities with an MSFS program in financial planning topics such as pensions and estate planning earn the MSFS.
- *Registered Representative* (reg. rep.)—Persons who pass the Series 7 exam and are licensed by the National Association of Securities Dealers (NASD) to sell securities earn the title registered representative.
- *The Registry*—The Registry of Financial Planning Practitioners is a voluntary distinction held by about 1,000 financial professionals nationwide who meet certain educational requirements, pass a written examination, have at least three years' experience in comprehensive financial planning, submit a written plan for review and receive at least 30 hours of continuing education per year.

Other facets of a planner's background should also be examined. Look for a degree in accounting, business administration, consumer education, economics or finance. Learn what areas a planner is particularly knowledgeable in and whether he or she concentrates on a particular type of client (e.g., farmers, dentists).

As is advisable for other services that consumers can purchase, shop around for a financial planner. Start by asking for recommendations from friends, relatives or other financial professionals with whom you do business. Then interview several planners. Request and examine closely a few plans developed by the planner for others. Some hallmarks of a good financial plan are clearly written sentences, easy-to-understand recommendations, a cash flow analysis, a net worth statement, an evaluation of current insurance protection, a tax analysis and a statement of goals, objectives and tolerance for investment risk.

Find out how long the planner has been in business and how he or she stays current with tax law changes and new investment products. Activity in professional associations is one indication of a planner's commitment to professional improvement. Insist on seeing proof of registration with, or licensing by, appropriate regulatory agencies. Planners who sell securities and receive compensation for investment advice should display evidence of registration with the NASD and the SEC. Those who handle insurance should be licensed by a state department of insurance or a comparable agency.

Be prepared to pay for the advice you receive from a financial planner. Get a written estimate of costs in advance. Financial planners can be paid in one of three ways. Some charge a set fee or an hourly rate, generally between $75 to $200 per hour, to prepare a written plan. Others do not charge a consulting fee but are compensated by commissions on the financial products (e.g., insurance policies) they sell. Still others are compensated both ways: a fee plus commissions. Some planners accept only high-income clientele with a designated net worth (e.g., $500,000). Others gear their services to the middle class.

Some financial planners provide a free first visit to get acquainted and to determine whether they can help you achieve your financial goals. It is important to know what sort of advice and information you want before arranging a consultation. Assemble in advance facts and figures regarding your financial situation. The better prepared you are when you see a financial planner, the more helpful and less costly a planner's advice could be.

12 Questions To Ask a Financial Planner

Listed below are questions that you should ask a financial planner during your initial visit. Although no set answers exist, responses can provide valuable information on which to base your decision.

① **What financial planning services can you provide for me?**—Many financial planners are specialists in a particular area, such as insurance, mutual funds or taxation. Try to determine whether they are also able to provide a broad range of services.

② **Will you have direct access to my money?**—Direct access to clients' funds creates a greater risk for clients and a greater liability for planners. Get details regarding the bonding and insurance the financial planner carries.

③ **Do you sell products in addition to your financial planning services?**—The sale of products, in addition to planning services, creates the *potential* for a conflict of interest. On the other hand, financial plans can sit on a shelf unheeded if a financial planner lacks the capacity to implement them. Implementation requires the sale of products. A conflict of interest occurs *only* when a planner takes actions that are detrimental to a client's interests but profit the planner.

④ **If you sell me a product that you recommend in the financial plan, how will you be compensated?**—It is important that all forms of compensation (fees, prizes, commissions, etc.) be fully and clearly disclosed before you enter into an agreement with a financial planner.

⑤ **What resources, staff and facilities do you have at your disposal?**—Financial planning requires a broad base of knowledge and expertise. One person cannot be an expert in all areas. Back-up personnel or networks with other professionals (e.g., attorneys, accountants) are vital to successful financial planning.

⑥ **After you develop my financial plan, what follow-up services can I expect?**—A financial planner should continue to work with you to monitor, update and revise your plan as necessary. Depending on your needs and situation, follow-up may occur monthly to annually.

⑦ **How will you be compensated for the development of my financial plan and for follow-up services?**—Disclosure of fees for planning and follow-up services should be full, detailed and clear before you enter into an agreement with a financial planner.

⑧ **In what ways will you assist me in the actual implementation of my financial plan?**—Many plans fail because the financial planner doesn't help beyond the initial plan development and clients hesitate to implement plans on their own. Someone (the financial planner or another financial services professional) should be involved in the implementation phase, usually with additional compensation for that function.

⑨ **What are your educational credentials and business experience?**—The broad areas involved in financial planning and the management of a successful practice require extensive education and experience.

⑩ **In what ways do you keep current with financial developments and changes in tax regulations?**—The dynamic nature and increasing complexity of financial planning demand the maintenance of a high level of professional competence. This is accomplished through programs of continuing education, subscription services, seminars and networking with one's peers and should be part of a financial planner's informational background.

⑪ **What licenses, certifications and registrations do you have?**—Ask about licenses and federal and state registration required of persons working in the financial services industry.

⑫ **Do you have a professional designation and membership in a professional organization in the financial field?**—Professional designations such as CLU, ChFC, CFP and CPA usually indicate a high level of interest in providing competent and ethical service to clients. Active membership in a professional organization also involves a continuing education program to keep members current in the field.

Be Your Own Financial Planner

In Chapter 2, the financial planning process was likened to preparations for traveling. With many trips, you can often take more than one route to your destination. You can choose the route that is the shortest, the cheapest or the most scenic. Any way you go, you will eventually arrive at your destination. Likewise, you have a number of different ways to reach your financial goals. People who have the time and expertise may wish to do their own financial planning. Frequent updating is necessary, however, to keep abreast of changes in the financial marketplace.

Figure 17.2 contains a worksheet that you can use to commit your financial plans to paper. Completing it will require a thorough understanding of your financial situation, an analysis of your financial goals (see Figure 2.2) and a calculation of your household cash flow (see Figure 4.2). The amount of savings needed to reach one or more financial goals is then compared to the amount of money available for saving and the goal(s) adjusted as necessary. The time value of money worksheet (see Figure 8.5) can be used to identify the amount of savings needed to achieve a goal over a given time period at a given rate of interest.

Completing this worksheet will also be helpful if you decide to work with a professional financial planner. Gathering the data needed for a financial analysis will make you a more knowledgeable client. One of the most difficult steps in the entire financial planning process is

collecting and organizing financial data and describing
your goals in detail.

Figure 17.2 Be Your Own Financial Planner—Worksheet

1. List up to five *strengths* of your current financial
   situation:

   • _____
   • _____
   • _____
   • _____
   • _____

2. List up to five *weaknesses* of your current financial
   situation:

   • _____
   • _____
   • _____
   • _____
   • _____

3. List steps that can be taken to turn your weaknesses
   into strengths:

Action	*Who Will Initiate or Assist?*
_____	_____
_____	_____
_____	_____
_____	_____
_____	_____

Figure 17.2 Be Your Own Financial Planner—Worksheet (Continued)

4. List up to five financial goals in a specific and quantifiable format (date, cost, etc):

   Example: Pay off $2,000 on Mastercard within one year

   - _____
   - _____
   - _____
   - _____
   - _____

5. List your goals in _order of importance:_

   - _____
   - _____
   - _____
   - _____
   - _____

6. Keeping the goals in priority order, list the _annual_ and _monthly_ savings required to achieve them:

Goal	_Annual Savings Amount_	_Monthly Savings Amount_
____	_____	_____
____	_____	_____
____	_____	_____
____	_____	_____
____	_____	_____

7. What is the total amount of money needed each month to fund the goals listed above? $_____

8. Checking your monthly cash flow worksheet, is it realistic that you can save the amount of money you need to reach your financial goals? yes_____ no_____

Figure 17.2 Be Your Own Financial Planner—Worksheet (Continued)

If so, congratulations! With a little work, you're on your way!

If not, rework your financial goals (e.g., extend the time frame, substitute a lower cost item, etc.)

9. List up to five strategies that you could use to save more money (see Chapter 5):

- _____
- _____
- _____
- _____
- _____

10. List up to five strategies that you could use to increase your income or reduce your expenses (see Chapter 6):

- _____
- _____
- _____
- _____
- _____

Whether you develop your own financial plan or pay someone for financial advice, you'll still need help implementing it. Numerous individuals and firms offer financial services, including bankers, lawyers, accountants, insurance agents and stock brokers. Many people employ a combination of advisers for specific aspects of their financial plan. The greater your income and assets, the greater the chance you'll need professional assistance, particularly for estate planning and tax preparation. Otherwise, you could risk overlooking errors and opportunities that an unbiased third party might have detected.

Hiring professional advisers with whom you share details of your financial life is a personal decision. Mostly, it boils down to how much time you have to spend on financial management and how much responsibility you are willing to turn over to others. If you're perpetually making New Year's resolutions to get your finances in order, perhaps it's time to consider the services of a financial planner.

Bibliography

A Consumer Guide to Financial Independence. Atlanta: International Association for Financial Planning, 1992.

A Profile of Older Americans: 1991. Washington, D.C.: American Association of Retired Persons, 1991.

Ahlburg, D., and G. DeVita. "New Realities of the American Family." *Population Bulletin* 47, no. 2 (August 1992).

Alessandra, M. "Women the Winners in the Investment Game." *Times-Picayune*, New Orleans (June 11, 1989).

"Annual Expenditures of All Consumer Units: Consumer Expenditure Survey, 1990." *Family Economics Review* 5, no. 2 (1992):22.

"Annuities." *Consumer Reports* (January 1988): 35–45.

Belsky, G. "The Five Ways Women Are Often Smarter Than Men about Money." *Money* (June 1992): 75–82.

Belsky, G., and B. Kobliner. "He Says, She Says: How Men and Women Differ about Money." *Money* (November 1993): 76–84.

Bernheim, B. D., *Is the Baby Boom Generation Preparing Adequately for Retirement? Summary report*. Princeton, N.J.: Princeton University, 1993.

Bernheim, B. D., and J. K. Scholz. "Do Americans Save Too

Little?" *Business Review*, Federal Reserve Bank of Philadelphia (September/October 1993): 3–20.

Bodnar, J. "Double Your Money." *Kiplinger's Personal Finance Magazine* (October 1992): 37–42.

Brennan, P., and B. O'Neill. "Starting out or Trading up: How to Buy a Home." *Rutgers Cooperative Extension Fact Sheets* #411–416 (1989).

Bresiger, G. "Personal Savings Rate Remains Anemic." *Financial Planning* (June 1993): 25–27.

Brown, W. "What Price, Peace of Mind?" *Financial Planning* (May 1989): 37–38.

CFP I: Introduction to Financial Planning. Denver: College for Financial Planning, 1982.

Checkoway, A. "Why and How To Select a Disability Policy for Your Clients." *Journal of Financial Planning* 3, no. 1 (1990): 24–27.

"Computing Your Risk Tolerance." *Money* (April 1988): 71.

"Consistency and Long-Term Planning Are Keys to Success." *Strategy for the Serious IRA/Keogh Investor.* New York: Shearson Lehman Brothers, January 1, 1988.

Consumer Handbook to Credit Protection Laws. Washington, D.C.: Federal Reserve System, 1989.

"Cost and Time Curtail Mall Shopping." *Wall Street Journal* (April 25, 1994): B1.

"Cost of Food at Home." *Family Economics Review* 7, no. 1 (1994): 43.

Clayton, G., and C. Spivey. *The Time Value of Money.* Philadelphia: W. B. Saunders Co., 1978.

Courtless, J. "Trends in Consumer Credit." *Family Economics Review* 6, no. 3 (1993): 8–17.

———. "Trends in Savings." *Family Economics Review* 4, no. 4 (1991): 15–21.

Credit Cards: What You Don't Know Can Cost You! Herndon, Va., Bankcard Holders of America, 1992.

Crispell, D. "Odds and Ends." *Wall Street Journal* (September 13, 1993): B1.

Davis, K. "Is Your Life Insuror Healthy? How To Read the Ratings." *Kiplinger's Personal Finance Magazine* (September 1991): 22–25.

Deacon, R., and F. Firebaugh. *Family Resource Management: Principles and Applications*. Boston: Allyn and Bacon, Inc., 1988.

Detweiler, G. "Credit Cards: What You Don't Know Can Cost You!" *Advancing the Consumer Interest* 5, no. 2 (1993), 6–11.

————. *The Ultimate Credit Handbook*. New York: Plume Books, 1993.

"Do Americans Need Financial Planners?" *Financial Planning* (October 1993): 40–45.

Dominguez, J., and V. Robin. *Your Money or Your Life*. New York: Penguin Books, 1992.

Dorfman, J. *The Mortgage Book*. New York: Consumer Reports Books, 1992.

Dugas, C. "Shopping Around for a Credit Card Could Pay Dividends." *Star Ledger,* Newark, New Jersey (August 9, 1993).

Dunton, L. *Spending by Choice: A Unique, Fun Way to Reduce "Buyer Remorse."* San Diego: National Center for Financial Education, 1992.

Eisenson, M. *The Banker's Secret*. New York: Villard Books, 1991.

Faber, R., and T. O'Guinn. "Compulsive Consumption and Credit Abuse." *Journal of Consumer Policy* 11 (1988): 97–109.

"Family Finances." *Family Economics Review* 5, no. 3 (1992): 28–30.

Farhi, P. "Number of U.S. Millionaires Soars." *Washington Post* (July 11, 1992): A1.

Feinberg, A. *Downsize Your Debt*. New York: Penguin Books, 1993.

"Financial Counseling." *Wall Street Journal* (February 24, 1994): A1.

Gallager, M. C. "The Tangled Coils of COBRA." *Financial Strategies* (Winter 1987): 55,86.

Garman, E. T., and R. E. Forgue. *Personal Finance*. Boston: Houghton Mifflin Co., 1994.

Goode, E. "On the Delicate Subject of Money." *U.S. News and World Report* (March 7, 1988): 68–69.

Greco, M. "Insurance Against Disability." *Star Ledger*, Newark, New Jersey, (May 8, 1992): NJI–12.

Hallman, G., and J. Rosenbloom. *Personal Financial Planning*. New York: McGraw-Hill Book Co., 1985.

Henry, E. "Charting a Course for Your 401(k)." *Kiplinger's Personal Finance Magazine* (March 1994): 95–99.

"Here Are the Averages for Itemized Deductions on 1991 Personal Returns." *Wall Street Journal* (June 16, 1993): B5.

Herman, T. "Preparing Your '93 Return May Prove Taxing." *Wall Street Journal* (February 18, 1994): C1, C6.

———. "With Clinton's New Tax Law, Business Travelers Have To Be Extra Vigilant." *Wall Street Journal* (March 28, 1994): B1.

Hogarth, J. "Choosing Financial Advisors." *Cornell Cooperative Extension Bulletin* (1987).

———. "Investment Basics." *Cornell Cooperative Extension Bulletin* (1987).

———. "Ready . . . Set . . . Retire." *Cornell Cooperative Extension Bulletin* (1987).

"Household Wealth and Asset Ownership: 1988." *Family Economics Review* 4, no. 4 (1991): 24–25.

"How To Choose a Credit Card." *Consumer Reports* (May 1990): 315.

"How To Handle a Windfall." *Consumer Reports* (June 1993): 361.

Huntley, H. "Making the Most of Your Money." *St. Petersburg Times* (September 1, 1986): IE, 10E.

"Investing for College." *Consumer Reports* (May 1994): 314.

Jorgensen, J. *It's Never Too Late To Get Rich*. Chicago: Dearborn Financial Publishing, 1994.

Kalmer, J. "Providing Adequate Disability Insurance." *Financial Services Times* (September 1987): 35.

Keeping Family/Household Records: What To Discard. Washington, D.C.: Superintendent of Documents, Circular YS–73–1.

Kleiman, C. *The 100 Best Jobs for the 1990s and Beyond*. Chicago: Dearborn Financial Publishing, (1992).

Kobliner, B. "Credit Cards That Pay You Back." *Money* (December 1993): 100–102.

Koretz, G. "Have Household Balance Sheets Improved That Much?" *Business Week* (April 12, 1993): 22.

Lawrence, J. *The Budget Kit*. Chicago: Dearborn Financial Publishing, 1993.

Leech, I., and E. Scott. "Insurance in General." *Virginia Cooperative Extension Publication* #354–022 (1991).

Leffler, W. "A New Model for Explaining Retirement Funding to Clients." *Mutual Fund News* 15, no. 3 (1993): 3, 6.

Leonard, F. "Pensions: Off Balance." *Modern Maturity* (October/November 1989): 78–81.

MacDonald, E. "How To Beat the 20% Withholding Trap." *Money* (February 1993): 62–65.

Maddux, E. "Household Records: What To Keep and Where." *Georgia Cooperative Extension Circular* #759–7 (1986).

———. "Your Money Matters." *Georgia Cooperative Extension Circular* #770 (1985): 1–6.

"Marriage Penalty." *Wall Street Journal* (May 11, 1994): A1.

Martin, M. E., and M. J. Martin. *Home Filing Made Easy!* Chicago: Dearborn Financial Publishing, 1994.

Matejic, D. "How Much Am I Worth?" *Rutgers Cooperative Extension Fact Sheet* #FS012 (1984).

———. "Programming My Dollars." *Rutgers Cooperative Extension Fact Sheet* #FS063 (1984).

———. "Sources of Retirement Income." *Rutgers Cooperative Extension Fact Sheet* newsletter insert (1985).

———. "Your Money Matters." *Rutgers Cooperative Extension Publication* #E.B. 424 (1979).

Matejic, D., B. O'Neill and G. Waranis. "Financial Planning for the Two-pay-check Family." Rutgers Cooperative Extension newsletter series (1981).

Matthews, A. "Marriage and the Other "M" Word—Money." *Money* (May 1988): 143–150.

McCormally, K. "Supercharge Your IRA." *Kiplinger's Personal Finance Magazine* (April 1994): 46–54.

Meyer, S. "Saving and Demographics: Some International Comparisons." *Business Review*, Federal Reserve Bank of Philadelphia (March/April 1992): 13–23.

Mitchell, G., and P. Zalenski. "Inflation, Recession, and Economic Change: How Some Virginia Households Adjusted." *Virginia Cooperative Extension Publication* #354–180 (1985).

Mittra, S. "Sizing up a Financial Planner." *Financial Planning* (August 1993): 22–28.

Money Matters. Washington, D.C.: American Association of Retired Persons, 1991.

Morris, B. "Big Spenders: As a Favorite Pastime, Shopping Ranks High with Most Americans." *New York Times* (July 30, 1987): 1, 13.

"1994 Annual Limits Relating to Retirement Planning." *NEFE Digest* (May 1994): 5.

"1992 Yearbook." Chicago: Ibbotson Associates, 1992.

O'Neill, B. "Beyond the Cookie Jar: Women's Changing Financial Needs." *Journal of Home Economics* 83, no. 2 (1991): 50–56.

———. "How Much Do I Need To Save for Retirement?" *Rutgers Cooperative Extension Fact Sheet* #FS431 (1989).

———. "Planning Ahead for the Cost of College." *Rutgers Cooperative Extension Fact Sheet* #FS634 (1992).

———. "Twenty-five Ways To Live on Less." *Rutgers Cooperative Extension Fact Sheet* #564 (1991).

——. "Twenty Ways To Save Money." *Rutgers Cooperative Extension Fact Sheet* #FS563 (1991).

"Paying More for Social Security." *Kiplinger's Personal Finance Magazine* (January 1994): 122.

"Payment of Household Debts." *Family Economics Review* 4, no. 4 (1991): 28–29.

Peck, C., and G. Webster. "Women and Pensions." *Journal of Home Economics* 77, no. 1 (1985): 10–15.

Proceedings of Personal Economic Summit '93. Denver: Institute of Certified Financial Planners, 1993.

Razzi, E. "Renting Out Your House." *Kiplinger's Personal Finance Magazine* (June 1994): 67–73.

Reid, J. "Cutting the Cost of Your Coverage." *Money* (April 1988): 68–69.

———. "It's Still Life Insurance, After All." *Money* (March 1987): 167–178.

Robertson, A. *Social Security: What Every Taxpayer Should Know.* Washington, D.C.: Retirement Policy Institute, 1992.

Rosewicz, B. "Choosing a Financial Planner." *Wall Street Journal* (1987): 39D, 41D.

Shilling, A. G. "The Next Crisis in the Banking Industry May Come from the Use of Credit Cards." *Los Angeles Times* (July 21, 1991): D2.

Skousen, M. *Scrooge Investing*. Chicago: Dearborn Financial Publishing, 1994.

"Sorting Through the Alphabet Soup." *CFP Today* (October 1993).

Staten, M. "Credit After Bankruptcy: A Problem of Incentives." *Credit World 79*, no. 7 (September/October 1991): 10–20.

Statistical Abstract of the United States 1993. Washington, D.C.: U.S. Department of Commerce, Bureau of the Census, 1994.

Stephenson, M. "Getting out of Debt." *Maryland Cooperative Extension Service Fact Sheet* #436 (1992).

―――. "Risk Management: Homeowners Insurance." *Maryland Cooperative Extension Service Fact Sheet* #437 (1987).

―――. "Risk Management: Life Insurance." *Maryland Cooperative Extension Service Fact Sheet* #371 (1987).

"Study By Displaced Homemakers Says Ranks Are Rising." *Star Ledger*, Newark, New Jersey (July 30, 1987): 12.

"Survey Shows Banks' Willingness to Waive Fees for Credit Cards." *Wall Street Journal* (September 12, 1991): B5.

Susswein, R. "Credit Card (Plasticard) Trends." *AFCPE Newsletter* 11, no. 2 (April 1994): 1–3.

"Tax Report." *Wall Street Journal* (December 15, 1993): A1.

Tengel, P. "Understanding Savings and Investments." *Maryland Cooperative Extension Fact Sheet* #442 (1988).

The Consumer's Guide to Estate Planning. Denver: College for Financial Planning, 1989.

The Consumer's Guide to Insurance Planning. Denver: College for Financial Planning, 1989.

The Dollarplan Financial Education Course. San Diego: National Center for Financial Education, 1986.

The National Foundation for Consumer Credit. Silver Spring, Md.: National Foundation for Consumer Credit, 1992.

The Social Security Book: What Every Woman Absolutely Needs To Know. Washington, D.C.: American Association of Retired Persons, 1991.

Topolnicki, D. "The Fine Art of Managing a Lump Sum." *Money* (December 1988): 109–111.

Topolnicki, D., and E. MacDonald. "The Bankruptcy Bonanza." *Money* (August 1993): 82–94.

"Treasury Says Sales of EE Savings Bonds Fell 52.1% Last Month." *Wall Street Journal* (February 10, 1994): B2.

Tritch, T. "Americans and Their Money." *Money* (March 1992): 72–75.

Turner, J. "99 Ways To Save Money." *Alabama Cooperative Extension Service Circular* #HE-562 (1990).

Understanding Social Security. Washington, D.C.: U.S. Department of Health and Human Services, Publication #SSA-10024, 1993.

Underwood, D., and P. Brown. *Grow Rich Slowly*. New York: Viking Books, 1993.

"USA Snapshot: Why People Seek Counseling for Debt Problems." *USA Today* (January 14, 1994): 1B.

"U.S. Families' Net Worth Fell 12% from '88 to '91." *Wall Street Journal* (January 26, 1994): B6.

Ventura, J. *The Bankruptcy Kit*. Chicago: Dearborn Financial Publishing, 1991.

———. *The Credit Repair Kit*. Chicago: Dearborn Financial Publishing, 1993.

———. *Fresh Start*. Chicago: Dearborn Financial Publishing, 1992.

Veres, R. "An Education in College Planning." *CFP Today* (October 1992): 8–13.

Waggoner, J. "Banks' Holiday Celebration: Plastic for a Song." *USA Today* (November 8, 1993): 3B.

"Wal-Mart Family Richest in America." *Star Ledger*, Newark, New Jersey (July 24, 1988): 8.

Walters, D. "Gender Gap Narrowing as Men's Pay Drops at Faster Rate Than Women's Pay." *Los Angeles Times* (September 13, 1992): D3.

What Happens When Someone Dies Without a Will? Name Your State. San Diego: National Center for Financial Education, 1988.

What To Do When You're Blessed With an Inheritance or Windfall. Atlanta: Committee for Financial Independence, 1986.

When Your Home Is on the Line: What You Should Know about Home Equity Lines of Credit. Washington, D.C.: Federal Reserve System, 1989.

"Where Does All the Money Go?" *Consumer Reports* (September 1986): 581–92.

Wilcox, M. "What To Do With a Big Cash Payout." *Kiplinger's Personal Finance Magazine* (January 1993): 53–56.

Women, Pensions, and Divorce. Washington, D.C.: American Association of Retired Persons, 1993.

Index

PUTNAM ⟨ρ⟩BERKLEY
online

Your Internet gateway to a virtual environment
with hundreds of entertaining and enlightening
books from the Putnam Berkley Group.

While you're there visit the PB Café and
order-up the latest buzz on the best authors and
books around—Tom Clancy, Patricia Cornwell,
W.E.B. Griffin, Nora Roberts, William Gibson,
Robin Cook, Brian Jacques, Jan Brett,
Catherine Coulter and many more!

Putnam Berkley Online is located at
http://www.putnam.com/berkley

• •

PUTNAM BERKLEY NEWS

Every month you'll get an inside look at our
upcoming books, and new features on our site.
This is an on-going effort on our part to
provide you with the most interesting and
up-to-date information about
our books and authors.

Subscribe to Putnam Berkley News at
http://www.putnam.com/berkley/subscribe